PRAISE FOR *MISSIONARY BAPTISM & EVANGELICAL UNITY*

"Missionary Baptism! Yes! . . . All you say is just right. The theologies can be harmonized, I believe. Jesus' final words were 'be one.' Cameron, you're doing it! Thank you."

—D. CLAIR DAVIS,
Professor of Church History emeritus, Westminster Theological Seminary, Philadelphia, Pennsylvania

"Believers' baptism and infant baptism are sometimes viewed in strong opposition to each other. However, this book narrows the divide and makes a case for a church accepting both approaches. I appreciate Cameron Fraser's warm heart for mission, conversion, and unity in Christ."

—DAVID J. FEDDES,
Provost, Christian Leaders Institute, and Pastor, Family of Faith CRC, Monee, Illinois

"Any future studies of baptism will need to take this one into account. I commend Cameron for his concern for unity."

—JOHN M. FRAME,
Professor of Systematic Theology and Philosophy emeritus, Reformed Theological Seminary, Orlando, Florida

"Dr. Cameron Fraser has written with his usual verve and vigor, clarity and conviction on a subject that is of perennial debate in the church. I warmly commend his contribution to the discussion. Even if you disagree with his conclusion, you will have had your mind stretched and heart warmed in the process."

—LIAM W. GOLIGHER,
Senior Minister, Tenth Presbyterian Church, Philadelphia, Pennsylvania

"If it has ever occurred to you that those practicing infant baptism have different and sometimes conflicting notions of what the sacrament means and accomplishes, then perhaps you will be ready to consider, with Cameron Fraser, that this discord exists because important fundamental questions have been neglected. Cameron ably adjudicates those questions here."

—KENNETH J. STEWART,
Professor of Theological Studies emeritus, Covenant College,
Lookout Mountain, Georgia

Missionary Baptism
&
Evangelical Unity

OTHER BOOKS BY J. CAMERON FRASER

Thandabantu:
The Man Who Loved the People

God Is Always Good: Cassidy's Story
(with Sonya M. Taekema)

A Personal Appreciation of D. A. Macfarlane

Developments in Biblical Counseling

Learning From Lord Mackay:
Life and Work in Two Kingdoms

Missionary Baptism
&
Evangelical Unity

An Historical, Theological, Pastoral Inquiry

J. CAMERON FRASER

*Forewords by Michael A. G. Haykin
and Angus Morrison*

WIPF & STOCK · Eugene, Oregon

MISSIONARY BAPTISM & EVANGELICAL UNITY
An Historical, Theological, Pastoral Inquiry

Wipf & Stock
An Imprint of Wipf and Stock Publishers
199 W. 8th Ave., Suite 3
Eugene, OR 97401

www.wipfandstock.com

PAPERBACK ISBN: 978-1-6667-2541-4
HARDCOVER ISBN: 978-1-6667-2047-1
EBOOK ISBN: 978-1-6667-2048-8

10/15/21

In memory of Lester Bauman (1954–2021)

"I have been reading books on this subject for the last forty-four years and more, and I know less about it now than I did at the beginning. Therefore, when I assert, and we must all assert, that we believe in baptism, for that is plainly commanded, yet we must not divide and separate over the age of the candidate or over the mode of administration."

D. MARTYN LLOYD-JONES
"WHAT IS AN EVANGELICAL?" (1971)

Contents

Permissions

Foreword

ALTHOUGH THERE WAS CONTROVERSY about the sacrament of baptism prior to the Reformation, the emergence of Anabaptism on the European continent in the sixteenth century, and then the rise of the Baptist movement in the British Isles in the following century, brought a level of controversy about this subject hitherto unprecedented. In the past five centuries, that controversy has not diminished, though thankfully it no longer involves physical force or lethal violence. While this irenic essay does not resolve the controversy, at least not for this convinced Baptist, it does suggest some fascinating possibilities.

Moreover, it reminded me that there have been Baptists in the past who sought to resolve this matter through infant dedication. Some contemporary Reformed Baptists have been extremely critical of this practice, but it has roots deep in the eighteenth century. For example, the Particular Baptist Maria de Fleury (fl. 1770–1790), who was descended from Huguenots, penned a couple of hymns for the dedication of infants in 1786. In one of them, she wrote:

> Father of Mercies, to thy feet,
> We come, in Jesu's name,
> Pleading the promise of thy grace,
> And merits of the Lamb.
>
> To us and ours the word descends,
> That brings salvation down;
> All that the Lord our God shall call,
> He will with glory crown.

Led by this hope, we venture near,
And bring our babes to thee:
O that they may, if so thy will,
Among that number be.

We would devote them to thy fear;
But, Lord, the work is thine:
O may thy Spirit fill their hearts,
With every grace divine.[1]

Maria's fabulous sentiments here did not bridge the "watery" gap between Paedobaptist and Baptist in the eighteenth century. And, for many, neither will this provocative essay. But what I love about this essay by J. Cameron Fraser is that it compels thought and reflection on the meaning of this central rite of the Christian faith. And in an age when ruffling feathers and injuring feelings are fast becoming taboo, that is a good thing.

MICHAEL A. G. HAYKIN, THD
Fellow of the Royal Historical Society; Chair and Professor of Church History & Director of The Andrew Fuller Center for Baptist Studies, The Southern Baptist Theological Seminary, Louisville, Kentucky; Professor of Church History, Heritage Theological Seminary, Cambridge, Ontario.

---

1. de Fleury, *Hymns for Believer's Baptism*, 20–21.

Foreword

HAVING READ WITH APPRECIATION Cameron Fraser's earlier articles on this topic in the *Scottish Bulletin of Evangelical Theology*, I welcome his treatment of the subject in this expanded form. It is a sad fact that, as with the Lord's Supper, baptism has occasioned much—at times bitter—controversy among Christian people. This has been notably the case in some debates between advocates of infant and of believers' baptism. At times more heat than light has been generated. Cameron's work, on the other hand, is marked by clarity and evenhandedness. He is motivated by a laudable desire to promote the unity of Christ's church, especially in its evangelical expression.

In a theological area in which a great deal hinges on careful conceptual nuancing, this study seeks to be fair to the many, often subtly differing, positions represented. An alert mind, it must be said, is required to follow what can be at times a rather confusing debate.

Cameron offers a fine example of the manner in which disagreements among Christians should be handled. Whether or not one agrees with every conclusion, we can all learn much from this insightful and irenic study.

THE VERY REV. ANGUS MORRISON, PHD, DD
Minister Emeritus, Orwell and Portmoak Parish Church,
Former Moderator, Church of Scotland,
Chaplain to HM the Queen in Scotland.

Preface

WHEN THE SHUTTLE DRIVER learned that I was a pastor in the Christian Reformed Church, he said, "So you believe that babies are born again by baptism." Well, not exactly, although this seems to be a common popular misunderstanding of infant baptism as practiced in Reformed churches. It is not without basis in at least some churches, but I want to argue that there is another way to understand Christian baptism that removes the basis for misunderstanding while promoting unity among evangelical (including Reformed) Christians. I am calling it *missionary baptism*, more commonly known as *household baptism*, following the pattern of New Testament baptisms that included at least a few baptisms of entire households, a pattern more common in missionary situations than in established churches.

The principles developed in this short book are ones I tried to practice in the early years of my first pastorate in the 1980s. I regret that I was not able to articulate them as clearly as I hope they are here. I am grateful to the longsuffering former members of Grace Reformed, Sechelt, BC, who endured my attempts to work through these issues with them.

Chapters 2, 3, and 4 of what follows originated as articles in the Spring and Autumn 2020 issues of the *Scottish Bulletin of Evangelical Theology*. I wish to thank the editor, the Rev. Dr. John Ferguson, for permission to reproduce them here in slightly modified and expanded form (plus Americanization!). Thanks also to Michael Haykin and Angus Morrison for their gracious forewords and encouragement along the way; one from each side of the Atlantic (although both originating from the same side), one a Baptist, the other a Presbyterian, illustrating the kind of unity being advocated.

I appreciate all others who read all or part of the manuscript, whether they responded positively or critically. All were of help. They include: Tom Albaugh, William Barker, Joel Beeke, D. Clair Davis, Blane Després, Bob Derrick, David Feddes, John Frame, Liam Goligher, Kristy Johnson, Robert (Bob) Letham, Calum MacIness, Ken Stewart, and John van Eyk. Most of all, my wife Margaret was, as always, my best critic and support. Additionally, Kristy Johnson provided valuable editorial help in areas where I am technologically challenged, and Jan Heetebrij helped by meticulously checking the index entries. Any remaining infelicities are my own.

My original working title was *Missionary Baptism and Christian Unity*, but I became increasingly concerned that it was open to the criticism that my definition of *Christian* was too narrow, since the unity I am seeking is with evangelicals who practice baby dedication and/or believers' baptism rather than with those of more liturgical paedobaptist traditions; and even then, my target audience is only a subset of those who identify as evangelical. I was hesitant to use *evangelical* because of the political baggage the term has come to be associated with, especially in the United States. Besides, the denomination to which I belong, and which provides much of the background to this study, has a history of distinguishing between *evangelical* and *Reformed*. I have written about this elsewhere, but *evangelical* is a label I am not yet prepared to give up (as some have). Properly and historically understood, it is a perfectly good description of biblical Christianity. A provocative 1995 article in the British publication, *Evangelical Quarterly* questions this, charging that evangelicalism is not properly Christian in its supposed isolation from the historic Christian tradition.[2] On the other hand, writing in 1978 of the Christianity "which we inherit from the New Testament via the Reformers, the Puritans, and the revival and missionary leaders of the eighteenth and nineteenth centuries," J. I. Packer added, "The reason why I call myself an evangelical and mean to

---

2. Letham and Macleod, "Is Evangelicalism Christian?," 3–33. Macleod's contribution is a response to Letham's argument.

go on doing so is my belief that as this historic evangelicalism has never sought to be anything other than New Testament Christianity, so in essentials it has succeeded in its aim."[3] Times have changed since 1978, but the truth of what evangelicalism has stood for historically has not.

I am grateful to several staff at Wipf and Stock for patiently guiding this project through the publication stage, as well as for promptly answering my questions. It is a privilege to be published by Wipf and Stock, who have, among other things, reprinted important classics on baptism by Kurt Aland, Karl Barth, G. R. Beasley-Murray, and Joachim Jeremias. I have benefited by reading their works, as well as others referenced in this study. Besides the formal permission notices from Authentic Media Ltd., and P & R Publishing, I am grateful for email permission to use:

- a substantial extract from David Feddes's Back to God Hour radio sermon, "Should Babies be Baptized?" Permission granted by Rev. Feddes and ReFrame (formerly Back to God) Ministries, 2002;

- an extract from Robert Letham's review of *The People's Theologian* in *Foundations* No. 61. Autumn 2011;

- a long quote from James B. Scott's article, "The Biblical Basis of Infant Baptism" from *New Horizons*, July-August, 2000.

- significant quotes from Dr. Joel R. Beeke's books, *Bringing Our Covenant Children to Christ* (Reformation Heritage, 2010) and *Parenting by God's Promises* (Reformation Trust, 2011);

- substantial use of *In Search of Ancient Roots* (Stewart, 2007) and *Baptism: Three Views* (Wright, 2009), as well as some quotations from *Christ, Baptism and the Lord's Supper* (Vander Zee, 2004), all published by InterVarsity (US).

Other quotations are either from works in the public domain or come under the "fair use" policies of the respective publishers. In accordance with Wipf and Stock's style guide, all footnotes (including the first mention of a publication) are provided in shortened

3. Packer, "Uniqueness of Jesus Christ," 102.

form, with a complete bibliography at the end of the book. Most books and articles are not listed in the index, as they can be found in connection with the names of the authors.

Thanks to Paul Fields, now Theological Librarian Emeritus, for help in tracking down older *Acts* and *Agendas of Synod* (unavailable online) at the Heckman Library, Calvin College and Seminary, Grand Rapids, Michigan.

I am dedicating this study to the memory of my Anabaptist friend Lester Bauman, with whom I shared more than the same birth year. He and I used to drive together to a monthly writers' guild meeting, which gave us ample opportunity to discuss the faith we held in common, and to learn from one another about our very different backgrounds. Lester was loyal to his Anabaptist heritage and, for historical reasons, would not have self-identified as an evangelical or even as a Protestant, but he was remarkably open to exploring differing perspectives, provided they were biblically based. His books are available on Amazon and elsewhere. He is missed.

1

A Highland Presbyterian
among the Dutch Reformed

THE IMMEDIATE STIMULUS FOR this study comes from my experience in two very different Reformed traditions; the Scottish (and specifically Highland) Presbyterianism of my background, and my years of pastoral ministry in the Christian Reformed Church in North America. The Highland tradition stressed the need for personal conversion and saw infant baptism as no more than a rite of admission into the visible church. More was required to participate in the Lord's Supper. For this, a person needed to give evidence of conversion. Thus, a distinction was made between those who were members in full communion and others who, though technically baptized members, were more generally referred to as adherents.

In the nineteenth century, noted Highland minister Dr. John Kennedy defended this view over against what he perceived to be the more liberal approach to church membership in the Lowland south.[1] (This distinction is no longer as clear-cut geographically as in Kennedy's day, but the issue remains.) Following the lead of Dr. John Macdonald, the famed "Apostle of the North," Kennedy distinguished between an *uncontradicted* profession of faith required for baptism and an *accredited* profession required for admission to the Lord's Table. In other words, a person who professed to believe

---

1. Kennedy, *Days of the Fathers*, 124–44.

in the Christian faith and lived an outwardly moral life would be eligible for baptism either for him or herself (if previously unbaptized) or their children. Evidence of a converted life and "marks of grace" were required for the further step of membership in full communion.

Kennedy sought to prove this to be the apostolic practice. He also identified his view with that of Petrus van Mastricht (1630–1706), one of the leaders of the seventeenth-century Dutch Further Reformation (*Nadere Reformatie*) which stressed the need for personal piety and experiential religion in addition to doctrinal orthodoxy and outward morality. Scotland experienced a similar movement at that time, the Second Reformation, corresponding to English Puritanism.

The *Nadere Reformatie* emphases continue in several branches of Dutch Reformed Christianity in the Netherlands, and the Netherlands Reformed Congregations in North America, as well as (since 1967) the Reformed Congregations in North America, and (since 1993) the Heritage Reformed Congregations (HRC), both splits from the Netherlands Reformed. A contemporary representative of this tradition and the best-known minister in the HRC, Dr. Joel R. Beeke, has written a short book called *Bringing the Gospel to Covenant Children*. He defines "covenant children" as "those children born to at least one confessing parent (1 Cor. 7:14), who are baptized and who are growing up in the community of the church, with all the riches and privileges that entails, such as being placed under the prayers of the church and the preaching, invitations and warnings of God's Word."[2]

These children are in need of evangelism, by which Beeke means

> presenting the gospel of Christ the Savior as the one thing needful in the lives of desperate sinners, including our covenant children, praying that by Spirit-worked faith and repentance they may be drawn to God through Christ, grow in Him, and serve Him as Lord in the

---

2. Beeke, *Bringing the Gospel*, 2.

fellowship of His church and the extension of His kingdom in the world.[3]

Beeke contrasts his view with that of those who *overestimate* the covenant relationship:

> This is particularly true of those who adhere to Abraham Kuyper's view of covenant children called "presumptive regeneration." Kuyper taught that the covenant warrants the presumption that the children of believers are regenerated from earliest infancy and possess saving grace unless they later reject the covenant. . . . Parents who presume that their children are regenerate by virtue of the covenant see no need to tell their children that they must be born again and come to repentance and faith in Jesus Christ.[4]

The Christian Reformed Church (CRC) tends to reflect Kuyper's influence in this as well as other respects, although it no longer *officially* endorses the Kuyperian doctrine of presumptive regeneration. A little historical background might help. The CRC has as its background the Reformed Churches in the Netherlands (*Gereformeerde Kerken in Nederland* [GKN], now part of the Protestant Church in the Netherlands) formed in 1892 by the merger of two groups that had broken away from the state church. The first group came from an 1834 secession known as the *Afscheiding* (which means "secession"). This movement stressed the need for conversion, personal piety, and separation from the world. The second group, which over time became more dominant, was under the leadership of theologian-turned-politician Abraham Kuyper (1837–1920), who served as Prime Minister of the Netherlands from 1901–05. Named the *Doleantie* (from the Latin *dolere*, to feel sorrow), this movement left the state church in 1886. It emphasized doctrinal orthodoxy, but also cultural engagement and Christian education in line with Kuyper's famous statement in a speech at the opening of the Free University of Amsterdam that "there is not

---

3. Beeke, *Bringing the Gospel*, 2–3.

4. Beeke, *Bringing the Gospel*, 4–5.

a square inch in the whole domain of our human existence over which Christ, who is Sovereign over all, does not cry, Mine!"[5]

Kuyper was a great and godly man, but he held some controversial views, including presumptive regeneration. This view was not original to Kuyper and has been traced back at least as far as the First Helvetic Confession of 1536.[6] According to Beeke, Kuyper was influenced by Gisbertus Voetius (1589–1676), also (like van Mastricht) of the Dutch Further Reformation; and in fact "widely regarded as the most advanced theological leader" of this movement.[7] It has been claimed that presumptive regeneration was also the view of John Calvin, as well as of Presbyterian orthodoxy.[8]

In 1905, the Synod of Utrecht of the GKN pronounced on this, among other Kuyperian distinctives:

> that according to the Confession of our Churches the seed of the covenant, by virtue of the promise of God, must be held to be regenerated and sanctified in Christ, until upon growing up they should manifest the contrary in their way of life or in doctrine;
>
> that it is, however, less correct to say that baptism is administered to the children of believers on the ground of their presumed regeneration, since the ground of baptism is found in the command and promise of God;
>
> that, furthermore, the judgment of charity with which the Church regards the seed of the covenant as regenerated, does not at all imply that each child is actually born again, seeing that God's Word teaches that they are not all Israel that are of Israel, and of Isaac it is said: in him shall thy seed be called (Rom. 9:6,7), so that it is imperative in the preaching constantly to urge earnest self-examination, since only he that believeth and is baptized shall be saved.[9]

5. Bratt, *Abraham Kuyper*, 488.

6. See Murray, *Christian Baptism*, 54n30.

7. Beeke, *Parenting by God's Promises*, 18.

8. See Schenck, *Presbyterian Doctrine*, ch. 1.

9. Christian Reformed Church, *Acts of Synod* 1908, 82–83.

The CRC was formed by Dutch immigrants to the United States in 1857, after they seceded from the Reformed Church in America that had been founded in 1754. The 1908 CRC adopted the findings of the Synod of Utrecht on presumptive regeneration and other matters. However, in 1962, it declared that these distinctives would not be held as a test of membership or holding office in the denomination. Then, in 1968, synod declared that the "Conclusions of Utrecht," as adopted in 1908, would no longer have the status of binding doctrinal deliverances. The reason given was not a rejection of presumptive regeneration and related doctrines as such; in fact, their value "in refuting certain errors in doctrine and life" was affirmed, if understood in their historical context, and ministers transferring into the CRC from other denominations were expected to respect them as such.[10] The motivating concern was rather one of paving the way for closer ties to two other denominations, one in the Netherlands (the *Christelijke Gereformeerde Kerken*, those congregations that had not taken part in the 1892 merger and reflected more the *Afscheiding* influence), the other in Canada (the Canadian Reformed Churches, whose roots go back to a 1944 split with the GKN when those ministers who rejected the Kuyperian view of the covenant were ejected).[11]

The careful wording of the "Conclusions of Utrecht," such that, "the judgment of charity with which the Church regards the seed of the covenant as regenerated, does not at all imply that each child is actually born again . . .," should mean that the doctrine of presumptive regeneration does not necessarily mean what Beeke states above; indeed, it should not and often does not. However, it can also lead to what a friend has called a "lazy presumptive regeneration" (meaning that parents leave the Christian nurture of their children almost exclusively to the church and Christian school). This can result in young people growing up in church, Sunday school, catechism class, and Christian school, making public profession of faith as a matter of course in their senior year of high school and then living a nominally Christian life without ever being

---

10. Christian Reformed Church, *Acts of Synod* 1968, 404.

11. These particular denominations are no longer pursuing relationships with the CRC, which has become a more mixed body than they are.

seriously challenged as to their need to "be born again and come to repentance and faith in Jesus Christ."[12] Even those who do become active Christians in the Kuyperian tradition, as one of their own number has confessed, "are more noted for their intellectual ability and culture-transforming zeal than for their personal godliness or their living relationship with Jesus Christ."[13]

Some who have grown up in the way described above and then come into contact with more conversion-oriented evangelical teaching (perhaps especially through the influence of the charismatic movement) discover that they were never truly born again in the first place and undergo a conversion experience, bringing them into a personal relationship with Jesus. One consequence of this can be a rejection of their infant baptism as a meaningless formality, a desire to be rebaptized and then to have their own children dedicated rather than baptized. Then there are church planters and other pastors of an evangelistic bent who see infant baptism as traditionally understood in the CRC as a barrier to new converts and other Christians who understand it to imply baptismal regeneration, and thus reject it. There has, accordingly, been a growing movement, especially among some church planters, to permit baby dedication in place of baptism.

In 1999, in response to a specific situation, I was asked to chair a committee of Classis Alberta South and Saskatchewan in preparing an overture that went to synod the following year, asking for a fresh study of baptism.[14] Specifically, we asked for greater clarity on the relationship between faith and baptism, a renewed emphasis on the sovereignty of God's grace as it pertains to baptism, and further discussion of continuity and discontinuity in the divine covenants. Synod showed a marked disinterest in reopening the issue, even though it was noted that the concerns of our overture resonated

---

12. See previous quotation from Beeke, *Bringing the Gospel*, 5.

13. Wolters, "What Is to Be Done?" para. 14.

14. The other committee members were the Revs. John Kerssies and Phil Reinders, with Mr. Al Brander. Reinders is now ministering in Ontario. Kerssies is retired in Ontario after having pastored there for a number of years. Brander is still in southern Alberta. Kerssies was the principal author of the overture.

with many of our church members. Several delegates, who spoke to me personally following the debate in which our overture was defeated, reinforced the impression that we had indeed raised an issue of considerable concern to at least some of our churches. I was encouraged to pursue the matter. That was over twenty years ago!

Meanwhile, Synod 2007 received an overture requesting guidance on the question of infant dedication as an alternative to baptism. This time, synod's response recognized that "More than forty years have passed since synod last addressed infant baptism. We live in a different day . . . and the churches would be well served by carefully considering questions not previously raised surrounding infant dedication, as well as be provided with a fresh articulation of the practice of infant baptism." The denomination's newly appointed Faith Formation Committee was tasked with providing biblical and pastoral guidance for councils that are "conversing with those members who are requesting infant dedication in place of infant baptism."[15] The committee presented a preliminary report to Synod 2011 that was then adopted as a final report in 2012.

As part of the background to its report, the committee "benefited by reviewing the history of credobaptism . . . and the Dutch Reformed tradition." After making the questionable assumption that "it appears that believer's baptism emerged quite late in church history," the report notes that

> not long after the Reformation there were baptistic influences in England and the European continent, and the Dutch Reformed churches worked hard to fend off their impact. . . . [A] soft spot for Baptists by those in the Dutch Reformed Churches can be traced at least back to the seventeenth century. . . . Without actually converting to the baptist position, there were experiential pastors of the *Nadere Reformatie* . . . who wrestled with the meaning of infant baptism.
>
> The *Nadere Reformatie* emphasis on personal experience was rediscovered in the *Afscheiding* of 1834 as believers read from the *Oude Schrijvers* (Old Writers) in their small group Bible studies. Some baptist tendencies

---

15. Christian Reformed Church, *Acts of Synod* 2007, 621.

tagged along on this spiritual renaissance, which also followed the church to the formation of the Christian Reformed Church in North America in 1857.

So it comes as no surprise that already in 1888, only 31 years after the denomination was founded here in the United States, there were questions in the church regarding the necessity of baptizing infants. When asked, synod responded unequivocally that year that parents who failed to present their children for baptism were to be "instructed and admonished patiently" and, that failing, were to be *disciplined.*

Synod's act indicates how seriously as a Reformed church we took the doctrine. Denying baptism to a covenant child was paramount to violating his or her covenant rights. Efforts to restrain baptist tendencies in the denomination were bolstered over the years by an influx of Kuyperian immigrants who leaned toward the teaching of presumptive regeneration. . . .

While there has never been an explicit prohibition in the confessions or Church Order against infant dedication, it was always understood as a practical denial of infant baptism.[16]

Synod 2012 commended the entire report to the churches and offered the following guidance:

When parents request infant or child dedication, the pastor and elders of local congregations should (1) engage in pastorally appropriate ways to celebrate the birth or adoption of the child, pray for the child and parents, and call for the commitment of the parents to nurture their children in the Lord; (2) engage in convicted and winsome teaching on the subject of infant baptism; and (3) refrain from leading rituals of infant or child dedication.[17]

While clearly rejecting any move to make dedication an alternative to infant baptism, there is evidence here of some movement

---

16. Christian Reformed Church, *Agenda for Synod* 2011, 613–14 (italics original).

17. Christian Reformed Church, *Acts of Synod* 2011, 831.

in terms of recognizing that it was and is becoming an issue, at least in some of our churches. Although a minority position, there are in fact churches that have not refrained from "leading rituals of infant or child dedication." One prominent pastor responded to an informal survey by saying, "Our church does 'Covenant Celebration and Dedication' when parents believe their children are included in God's covenant, and promise to bring them up in the Lord's training but still believe that baptism should occur after a personal profession of faith." Another stated that "while we do not do dedications, we also don't hold too strictly to the requirement that we baptize children of believing parents when the parents become members." This clearly differs from the older practice (thankfully no longer required) of disciplining those who refused to bring their children for baptism. The requirement seems to have been based on the assumption that such a refusal was due to a lack of understanding that could be rectified by adequate teaching, so that persistent refusal became a form of sinful rebellion. In some cases, perhaps many, teaching could certainly help clear up misunderstandings, but it is surely presumptuous to assume that this would necessarily be the reason for persistent rejection of the teaching.

The truth is that there are a variety of confusing interpretations of infant baptism among those who practice it.[18] These range from baptismal regeneration—as typically understood or in revisionist forms (see chapter 3 for both)—presumptive regeneration, presumptive election (see later), covenant baptism,[19] to what has been described (usually critically, sometimes contemptuously)

---

18. Hoeksema in *Believers and Their Seed* observes that "We must immediately remark that there has never been any unanimity about this subject among Reformed people. In fact, it cannot even be said that there is a single covenant conception which has won for itself the exclusive name of Reformed in distinction from all other views" (13).

19. This can include any of the previous views, but can also mean that the covenant sign of baptism, corresponding to the Old Testament sign of circumcision, is applied to the children of believers without any assumptions about their spiritual status, simply because they are partakers of the covenant of grace made with Abraham and renewed in Christ. Some Reformed Baptists describe their view as covenant baptism, but with a different meaning (to be discussed later).

as "baby dedication with water." Believers' baptism seems much simpler and more straightforward. As indicated in the preface, there are some Baptists and other evangelicals who seem to assume that those who practice infant baptism believe that the ceremony automatically means recipients are born again. This is true of the Roman Catholic ritual, although regeneration thus conferred may subsequently be lost and then restored by penance.[20] It is also true to varying degrees, at least in terms of the language used, in Lutheran, Anglican, and Methodist communions.[21]

Reformed theology generally rejects such a view, but often struggles to explain the difference. This essay will argue that a theory and practice closer to "baby dedication with water" safeguards against misunderstanding and, further, that a dual practice of infant baptism and baby dedication promotes the unity of Christ's church. (Michael Haykin, in the foreword, speaks of "infant dedication" as an alternative to infant baptism. The synod reports referenced above use both "infant" and "child" dedication. However, most of my Baptist friends prefer "baby dedication" and so this is the term I will use.) I first turn back to an understanding of infant baptism slightly different from the Highland one described above, but also part of my Scottish Presbyterian background, one which Highland ministers such as John Kennedy considered to be the Lowland view. It is based on the writings of nineteenth-century theologian William Cunningham, which I compare to what I am calling missionary baptism. I then turn back to the Dutch Reformed tradition and to Joel Beeke in particular, before attempting some final thoughts on the implications of all this for evangelical Christian unity. But first, what exactly is missionary baptism?

---

20. See *Catechism of the Catholic Church*, Part Two, Section Two, Chapter One, Article 1, para 1213; Chapter Two, Article 4, para 1446.

21. See Kolb, "God's Baptismal Act," 91–109. Kolb references Anglican and Methodist as well as Lutheran formularies, although he also notes differences of interpretation. The term *christening* used for infant baptism in some traditions (although strictly speaking it refers to the naming of the child) is usually understood to mean the child is now a Christian.

2

What Is Missionary Baptism?

KENNETH J. (KEN) STEWART's *In Search of Ancient Roots* includes
a chapter on "Early Church Baptism in the Hands of Evangelical
Protestants." It is based on the independent research of Everett F.
Ferguson and the late David F. Wright (1937–2008) into the practice
of baptism in the early church. Ferguson is an emeritus professor
of Abilene Christian University, Texas. He has "long been associated with the Christian Churches, one distinctive tenet of which
is that forgiveness of sins and the gift of the Holy Spirit is tied to
the administration of baptism—that is, baptism upon profession."[1]
Without in any way discounting his massive research into the
subject, it might be fair to say that he would have been predisposed
to draw conclusions consistent with his own doctrinal beliefs.
Wright, on the other hand, presents a different picture. He grew up
in the Anglican communion and was for several years an elder in
the paedobaptist Church of Scotland, while teaching in the Church
History department of New College, University of Edinburgh.
He took the unusual position that paedobaptism was doctrinally
defensible but historically questionable. As Stewart notes, "It
may be fairly said that Wright wrote as one *not* motivated to see
the baptism of infants uprooted and removed but reformed and

---

1. Stewart, *In Search of Ancient Roots*, 128.

practiced on a principled basis in a setting in which indiscriminant (*sic*) infant baptism was and is rife."[2]

Among several points Stewart makes summarizing the research of both Wright and Ferguson are the following:

- "Infants suffering from life-threatening conditions probably provided the occasion that made baptism seem appropriate for the very young. (However, implicit in this practice was a notion that most Protestant Christians do not endorse: the absolute necessity of the reception of this sacrament[3] for salvation) . . . .

- "Under all normal circumstances, early Christian baptism followed extensive catechetical training ensuring that the baptismal questions were answered by instructed persons. As it was practiced and spread, infant baptism employed the same questions as previously, yet directed these questions to parents or sponsors of the infants."[4]

The first of these points has been questioned. John C. (Jack) Collins takes issue with Ferguson on the issue of emergency baptisms for sick and dying infants and suggests that his proposal that this is the origin of infant baptism "leads him to read the evidence in odd ways. . . . Ferguson's case for the aberrant origin of infant baptism sounds like special pleading."[5] Anthony (Tony) Lane also states that it would be wrong to conclude from the

---

2. Stewart, *In Search of Ancient Roots*, 128 (italics original).

3. The term *sacrament* is nowhere used in Scripture, and is thought to be derived from a Roman soldier's oath of allegiance (Tertullian), as an outward sign of an inward grace (Augustine). It is also indirectly derived from the Greek New Testament *mysterion* (mystery) *via* ecclesiastical Latin's *sacramentum* from *sacro* (sacred). Evangelicals often prefer to speak rather of an ordinance, in reaction to sacramentalism (the belief, opposed here, that the sacraments are intrinsically effective for salvation). The Westminster Shorter and Larger Catechisms define a sacrament as "a holy ordinance," thus covering both bases, but they also include the Word and prayer as ordinances.

4. Stewart, *In Search of Ancient Roots*, 131–32. Cf. Ferguson, *Baptism in the Early Church*, 355–57; Wright, *What Has Infant Baptism Done to Baptism?*, chs. 1 & 2.

5. Collins, "What Does Baptism Do?" 91–92.

inscriptional evidence of baptism taking place near the time of death that "infants were baptized *only* in case of emergency." The *Apostolic Tradition*, Tertullian, and Cyprian "all bear witness to the practice of infant baptism outside of the emergency context."[6] Sinclair Ferguson, referring to the inscriptional evidence cited by his namesake to the effect that "widespread infant baptism actually grew out of the practice of clinical baptism," notes that "this strand of evidence belongs to the period when baptism was already being postponed through fear of the risk of postbaptismal sin. It is doubtful if any concrete, rather than speculative, conclusions can be drawn from it."[7] However, as we shall see, the second point made above is supported by the historical evidence of the early (although seemingly not the apostolic) church.

Stewart summarizes some traditional arguments for infant baptism, admitting to "a sense of chagrin that standard authors writing to advocate infant baptism have found so little to discourage them in the meagreness of such historical materials."[8] There appear to be three possible responses: "*Disregard the problem of patchy historical evidence.* To date this seems to be the prevailing (though not exclusive) response from the conservative Protestant community that still upholds infant baptism. . . . *Abandon infant baptism altogether. . . . Modify infant baptism.*"[9] Under this last point, which Stewart favors, there are three further possibilities:

- *Make it an option for the children of those who request it.* "This is the line taken by the highly regarded A.N.S. (Tony) Lane in the recent volume *Baptism: Three Views.*"[10] There is arguably supporting evidence in the early church. Lane also references a group of Baptist churches in seventeenth-century England "which began to accept either practice," and adds that "the church at Bedford, now named after Bunyan, has maintained

---

6. Wright, *Baptism*, 151 (italics original).

7. Wright, *Baptism*, 79.

8. Stewart, *In Search of Ancient Roots,* 133.

9. Stewart, *In Search of Ancient Roots,* 133–35 (italics original).

10. Wright, *Baptism*, 139–71.

this approach down to the present day."[11] Then there are nineteenth-century examples, as well as present-day denominations that at least in theory, if not always in practice, take this view. Lane mentions two American-based churches, the Evangelical Covenant Church and the Church of the Nazarene. Stewart adds the Evangelical Free Church of America (and Canada) which has "historically provided for such a dual-baptism policy but has largely allowed the baptism of infants to vanish."[12]

- *"Defend infant baptism on grounds that hitherto have not been used"* (an unlikely prospect).

- *"Defend the baptism of infants by a renewed attention to the household baptisms of Acts 16 and 1 Corinthians 1:16."* Here

---

11. Wright, *Baptism*, 165. Cf. Pearse, *Great Restoration,* 212–13. Historians have debated whether John Bunyan (1628–88) was himself a "true" Baptist or a Congregationalist with credobaptist beliefs. See Finn, "Was John Bunyan a Baptist?," paras. 8, 3. According to Finn, Bunyan "was an Independent Baptist who practiced open membership and open communion. While this was a minority position, it was not unknown among British Baptists." Significantly, for purposes of this study, Finn adds, "For the past century, this exact position has been quite common among Baptists in the British Isles and Australasia (and, increasingly, in North America)." But Finn also states that "after Bunyan's death in 1688, the church gravitated toward mainstream Congregationalism and rejected credobaptism as a normative practice." This appears to contradict what Lane says above. The Rev. Chris Bamforth Damp, the current minister of Bunyan Meeting, sheds light on this in a May 16, 2021 email: "I don't think that Bunyan Meeting has ever really identified itself as a Baptist church. When we bought our current site in 1672—22 years after the formation of the church— the meeting house was registered as a Congregational meeting and Bunyan was registered as a Congregational preacher. The church could have registered as Baptist but did not and identified as Congregational. Bunyan himself identified as Congregational rather than Baptist and so this tradition was current during Bunyan's time at Bedford and was not a new innovation following his death in 1688. . . . So I suppose today, we take the view that we are a Congregational church and practice both forms of baptism—although I find that the vast majority of our baptisms are infants and only on two occasions in the last twenty years have we baptised a believer by immersion."

12. Stewart, *In Search of Ancient Roots,* 136. Cf. Wright, *What Has Infant Baptism Done to Baptism?*, 16.

Stewart references the work of the German scholar Joachim Jeremias in *The Origins of Infant Baptism* (1962).[13]

Stewart suggests that a doctrine which cannot be demonstrated to be universally held throughout church history should not be considered a primary doctrine of the faith. In drawing his argument to a close, he challenges his fellow paedobaptists with the question, "What would it require of us to see infant baptism occupy this more modest place in our churches today?" The answer is

> We would need to commit ourselves to reversing the proportions of those baptized in infancy (the vast majority in today's paedobaptist churches) and those baptized out of the world (the clear minority today). Does not the very frequency with which infant baptism is practiced in our churches practically obscure our failure to evangelize and baptize from the world?[14]

The position here advocated I am calling *missionary baptism* (not to be confused with the Missionary Baptist denomination). Others call it *converts' baptism*, which means essentially the same thing.[15]

Stewart goes on to quote with approval the nineteenth-century Scottish theologian James Bannerman (1807–68), who wrote:

> The true type of Baptism, from examining which we are to draw our notions as to its nature and efficacy, is to be drawn from the adult Baptisms in the early days of Christianity and not in the only Baptism now commonly performed in the professing church, the Baptism of infants. . . . Both among the enemies and friends of infant baptism the neglect of this distinction has been the occasion of numberless errors in regard to the import and effects of the sacrament. It is abundantly obvious

---

13. Stewart, *In Search of Ancient Roots*, 136–38 (italics original). Cf. Jeremias, *Origins of Infant Baptism*. This is "a further study" in reply to Aland's *Did the Early Church Baptize Infants?* Jeremias's first work on the subject was *Infant Baptism in the First Four Centuries*.

14. Stewart, *In Search of Ancient Roots*, 139.

15. See Wright, *Infant Baptism*, 362–76. Also, Wright, *Baptism*, 143, where Lane asserts, "What we see in Acts is not *believers'* baptism but *converts'* baptism" (italics original). Cf. Beasley-Murray, *Baptism in the New Testament*, 393–94.

that adult Baptism is the rule and infant Baptism the
exceptional case . . .[16]

Bannerman goes on to say of the baptized infant, that while
baptism "constitutes the door of admission into that visible Church
of God on earth of which the parent himself is a member . . . it
does not constitute him a member of the kingdom of heaven, but it
brings him to the very door, and bids him there knock and it shall
be opened unto him." Baptism gives infants "a right of property in
the covenant of grace; which may in after life, by means of their
personal faith, be supplemented by a right of possession."[17]

Bannerman was by no means alone among Scottish theologians in taking this position. Another (among several) was "Scotland's greatest theologian,"[18] William Cunningham (1805–61), who
was successively Professor of Theology, Professor of Ecclesiastical
History, and Principal of New College, Edinburgh. Cunningham
pointed out that missionaries generally experience more adult baptisms than those in more established churches that practice infant
baptism, and that if we were more familiar with this practice in our
churches, we would have a better understanding of the normativity
of such baptisms.[19] This essay will explore some of the implications
that arise from such a view. (The baptism of new believers is not
necessarily synonymous with *adult baptism*, but Cunningham consistently speaks of adults and so will the following exposition of his
views.)

---

16. Bannerman, quoted in Stewart, *In Search of Ancient Roots,* 139–40.

17. Bannerman, *Church of Christ,* 2:113–14.

18. The title of "Scotland's greatest theologian" is given to Cunningham by
Donald Macleod, principal emeritus of what is now the Edinburgh Theological
Seminary (formerly Free Church College). (See "Scotland's Greatest Theolo-
gian"; cf. Campbell and Maclean, *People's Theologian,* 65).

19. Cunningham, "Zwingli and the Sacraments," 246. Originally published
as an article in *the British and Foreign Evangelical Review,* October 1860.

3

William Cunningham and Missionary Baptism

William Cunningham was born on the 2nd of October, 1805, in the town of Hamilton in southwest Scotland. On the last day of 1810, his father received a fatal injury from falling off a horse and died soon after. William and his two younger brothers were raised in relative poverty by their widowed mother. He soon developed a reputation as an avid reader and for academic brilliance, coupled with modesty and personal loyalty, refusing on one occasion to name his fellow pranksters, even when threatened with jail by the Duke of Hamilton! Years later, the widow of a boyhood friend wrote to a member of the Cunningham family, "I have often heard my husband say that of all men he ever knew, Dr. Cunningham was the most essentially true, single-hearted and thoroughly unselfish. These are what we have all felt to be his crowning qualities—exemplified in a thousand ways."[1]

The family found it necessary to move three times during William's childhood, and it was in the town of Dunse, where relatives of his mother lived, that at the age of thirteen he offered to take over the regular practice of leading family worship. He also decided early on to become a minister, and it was with this in view that he

---

1. Rainey and Mackenzie, *Life of William Cunningham, DD*, 17.

attended the University of Edinburgh, first in its Faculty of Arts, then the Divinity Hall.

This was a period in which the Church of Scotland ministry was divided between moderates and evangelicals. The moderates were considered to be theologically orthodox, but preached morality more than credal Christianity and the need for regeneration by the Holy Spirit leading to a converted life. They also supported the system of patronage, by which parish ministers were appointed by landowners rather than called by the congregations. Cunningham began his studies as a moderate, but during his fourth term at the university he underwent a spiritual change and became an evangelical. Following his ordination, he served two pastorates, in Greenock and at Trinity College Church, Edinburgh. Then in the 1843 Disruption, he became a founding member, along with Thomas Chalmers, Robert Candlish, and others, of the Free Church of Scotland, largely over the patronage issue.

Towards the end of 1843, Cunningham traveled to America, where he received an honorary doctorate from Princeton University and went on to raise support for the new denomination. He was appointed Professor of Theology at New College, Edinburgh, before transferring to the chair of Church History in 1845. He succeeded Thomas Chalmers as Principal in 1847 and remained in this position until his death in 1861. Cunningham also served as moderator of the Free Church General Assembly in 1849.

William Cunningham was a good friend of Princeton Seminary theologian Charles Hodge (1797–1878). According to John Macleod (1872–1948) in his *Scottish Theology*, each considered the other "the foremost Reformed divine of their day."[2] However, one area of disagreement between Cunningham and Hodge would have been over the status of baptized children. Hodge held that since God's covenant promise "is not only to parents, but to their seed, children are by the command of God to be treated and regarded as of the number of the elect, until they give undeniable evidence to the contrary."[3] This differs only slightly from the view known

---

2. Macleod, *Scottish Theology*, 269–71.

3. Hodge, "Church Membership of Infants," 375–76.

as presumptive regeneration. Whereas Kuyper and others taught that baptized children should be presumed to be regenerate until and unless they proved otherwise, Hodge based the presumption on the doctrine of election rather than regeneration. Thus, a child might be presumed to be elect, but not necessarily yet regenerate.[4] In either case, the child was considered to be a child of God until proven otherwise.

Both presumptive election and presumptive regeneration seek to make the same judgment on the state of baptized children as is made of professing believers. We cannot read the hearts of believers, but can and must only take their outward profession as evidence of election and regeneration. The same judgment of charity is applied to their children before they are capable of professing or rejecting faith. This results from understanding the meaning of baptism as applying equally to believers and their children.

Cunningham disagreed. He believed that the biblical and confessional model was of adult (or believers') baptism and that infant baptism, while defensible in its own right, was a modification of adult baptism. Other than that infant baptism does not require infant faith, he nowhere says exactly what this modification consists of, but he likely would have agreed with his contemporary James Bannerman (quoted earlier), in distinguishing between a "right of property" and "a right of possession."[5]

CUNNINGHAM'S DOCTRINE OF BAPTISM

As Michael W. Honeycutt observes in "William Cunningham and the Doctrine of the Sacraments," Cunningham's approach to church history (or perhaps more accurately, historical theology) was to "hold past theological discussions up to the 'lamp of divine truth' to determine the extent to which they concurred with the 'unerring

---

4. Hodge, like Kuyper, was a man not only of great learning but of great piety, who understood the need for personal experience and could in no way be charged with presumption in the sense of taking one's election for granted. See e.g., Hoffeker, *Piety and the Princeton Theologians*.

5. See Bannerman, *Church of Christ* 2:113–14.

standard of the Word of God.'"[6] Thus, Cunningham was unasham-
edly polemical in his approach. This becomes apparent in his study
of the sacraments, where much of his polemic is directed against
the Roman Catholic doctrine and that of the Tractarians (or Oxford
Movement) of his day. However, there is much of abiding relevance
in Cunningham's approach to the subject, precisely because his
principal concern was as Honeycutt describes it.

Volume 2, chapter 22 of Cunningham's *Historical Theology*
is on "The Sacramental Principle." It moves from a discussion of
sacramental grace in general to baptismal regeneration, to infant
baptism in particular. In the first section, Cunningham notes that:

> The essential idea of [the] Popish and Tractarian doctrine
> of the sacraments is this: that God has established an in-
> variable connection between these external ordinances,
> and the communication of Himself—the possession by
> men of spiritual blessings, pardon and holiness; with
> this further notion, which naturally arises from it, that
> He has endowed these outward ordinances with some
> sort of power or capacity of conveying or conferring the
> blessings with which they are respectively connected.[7]

This leads to a study of baptismal regeneration, understood
as the idea that water baptism has an intrinsic power *ex opere operato* to effect justification and regeneration.[8] By way of contrast,

---

6. Campbell and Maclean, *People's Theologian*, 110.

7. Cunningham, *Historical Theology*, 2:124.

8. More recent ecumenical discussions of *ex opere operato* ("from the work
worked") suggest that it means only that the sacraments derive their power
from Christ's work rather than from humans. This is reflected in the most
recent *Catechism of the Catholic Church,* which states that the sacraments are
effective "by virtue of the saving work of Christ, accomplished once for all
. . . independently of the personal holiness of the minister. Nevertheless, the
fruits of the sacraments also depend on the disposition of the one who receives
them" (Part 2, Section One, Chapter One, Article 2, para 1128). There is evidence from church history that the term was originally intended to "safeguard
the sacraments from the heresies of Pelagianism (the notion that our works
of faith merit salvation) and Donatism (the notion that the efficacy of the
sacraments depended on the qualities of the officiant)" (Vander Zee, *Christ,
Baptism and the Lord's Supper,* 65). However, by the time of the Reformation,
it had come to be understood that the sacraments were automatic dispensers

"Protestants in general . . . regard the sacraments as signs and seals of the covenant of grace, signifying and representing in themselves, as symbols appointed by God, Christ and his benefits, operating beneficially only in those in whom faith already exists."[9] In other words, both baptism as the sacrament of initiation into the covenant of grace and the Lord's Supper as the sacrament of spiritual nurture presuppose the existence of faith in those who receive them. If this is the case, then how is one to understand the practice of infant baptism, when the infant is psychologically and developmentally incapable of a previous reception of Christ and his benefits by faith? It is to this and related questions that Cunningham devotes the remainder of the chapter.

Cunningham held that the New Testament model is adult baptism and that infant baptism, defensible in its own right on biblical grounds, is (as noted above) a modification of adult baptism. He also argued that the Westminster divines who gave us the Confession of Faith with the Larger and Shorter Catechisms had adult baptism in mind when they formulated their definitions of the sacraments in general and baptism in particular. He believed that:

> If we were in the habit of witnessing adult baptism, and if we formed our primary and full conceptions of the import and effects of the ordinance from the baptism of adults, the one sacrament would be as easily understood, and as definitely apprehended, as the other; and we would have no difficulty in seeing how the general definition of the sacraments in our Confession of Faith and Catechisms applied equally to both. But as this general definition of the sacraments, and the corresponding general description given of the objects and effects of

of grace, which is how the Reformers and the Reformed tradition, of which Cunningham was a part, understood the term. The Council of Trent, to which Cunningham was responding, stated in Session 7, Canon 8, "If anyone saith that by the said sacraments of the New Law grace is not conferred through the act performed but that faith alone in the divine promise suffices for the obtaining of divine grace: let him be anathema." In the Roman Catholic understanding, regeneration and justification can be lost by mortal sin, but restored as a result of penance.

9. Cunningham, *Historical Theology,* 2:134.

baptism, *do not apply fully and without some modification* to the form in which we usually see baptism administered, men commonly, instead of considering distinctly what are the necessary modifications of it, and what are the grounds on which these modifications rest, leave the whole subject in a very obscure and confused condition in their minds.[10]

In a wide-ranging essay, "Zwingli and the Sacraments," Cunningham credits Huldrych Zwingli (1484–1531) with having thrown off "the huge mass of extravagant absurdity and unintelligible mysticism, which from a very early period had been gathering round the subject of the sacraments, and which had reached its full height in the authorized doctrine of the Church of Rome."[11] According to Cunningham, "The Reformed confessions and Protestant divines, in general, have agreed very much in the definition or description of the sacraments, though there is a considerable diversity in the clearness and distinctness with which their doctrine is unfolded."[12] Zwingli's views were a reaction to Rome's, but other Reformers reacted against Zwingli with phrases that "approximate somewhat in phraseology to the Romish position."[13]

Coming more particularly to the subject of baptism, Cunningham first quotes the Westminster Shorter Catechism's general definition of a sacrament as "a holy ordinance instituted by Christ, wherein by sensible signs, Christ and the benefits of the new covenant are represented, sealed, and applied to believers."[14] He then

---

10. Cunningham, *Historical Theology*, 2:145 (italics original).

11. Cunningham, "Zwingli and the Sacraments," 228.

12. Cunningham, "Zwingli and the Sacraments," 239–40.

13. Cunningham, "Zwingli and the Sacraments," 240. Zwingli is generally understood to have had only a memorialist view of the sacraments as "bare and naked signs." Cunningham opines that "there are undoubtedly statements in Zwingli's writings which seem fairly to imply, that this was the whole doctrine that he taught concerning the sacraments." However, "there is some ground to think that, towards the end of his life, he ascribed a higher value and greater efficacy to these ordinances than he had once done" (226–27). This begs the question: Was Zwingli a Zwinglian in the sense that this designation is intended?

14. Cunningham, "Zwingli and the Sacraments," 242. Cf. Shorter Catechism, Q & A 92.

notes that "It is of fundamental importance to remember, that the Catechism does apply this whole description of a sacrament to baptism, and to realize what this involves."[15] The Catechism's definition of baptism is, "Baptism is a sacrament, wherein the washing with water, in the name of the Father, the Son and the Holy Ghost, doth signify and seal our ingrafting into Christ, our partaking of the covenant of grace, and our engagement to be the Lord's."[16] Cunningham observes:

> Now the only ground for alleging that this teaches baptismal regeneration, must be the notion, that it applies in point of fact to all who have been baptized, and that all who have received the outward ordinance of baptism are warranted to adopt this language and apply it to themselves. But the true principle of interpretation is, that this description of baptism fully and in all its extent applies only to those who are possessed of the necessary qualifications or preparations for baptism and are able to ascertain this. . . . Much evidently depends on the use and application of the pronoun *our* here. . . . The *our*, of course, suggests a *we* . . . and the question is, Who are the *we*?[17]

This question, says Cunningham, "is similar to that which is often suggested in the interpretation of the apostolic epistles, where the use of the words *we, us* and *our*, raises the question, Who are the *we*?"[18] The answer lies in taking the entire context into account. When this is applied to the Westminster standards, it becomes clear that the sacraments are for the benefit of believers. Understanding this brings clarity to the issue and it becomes apparent that the statement that "Baptism signifies and seals our ingrafting into Christ etc." must refer to "THOSE OF US who have been ingrafted into Christ by faith." This "removes all appearance of the Catechism teaching baptismal regeneration."[19] Cunningham continues:

---

15. Cunningham, "Zwingli and the Sacraments," 242–43.

16. Shorter Catechism, Q & A 94.

17. Cunningham, "Zwingli and the Sacraments," 243 (italics original).

18. Cunningham, "Zwingli and the Sacraments," 243(italics original).

19. Cunningham, "Zwingli and the Sacraments," 244 (italics original).

This mode of contemplating the ordinance of baptism is so different from what we are accustomed to, that we are apt to be startled when it is presented to us and find it somewhat difficult to enter into. It tends greatly to introduce obscurity and confusion into our whole conceptions on the subject of baptism, that we see it ordinarily administered to infants, and very seldom to adults. . . . Adult baptism, then, exhibits the original and fundamental idea of the ordinance, as it is usually brought before us, and as it is directly and formally spoken about in the New Testament.[20]

This is not to say that Cunningham found no biblical warrant for infant baptism. In his *Historical Theology*, he summarizes the evidence in reasonably typical paedobaptist fashion: noting the continuity and expansion of God's gracious dealings with children from the old covenant into the new, the federal holiness of the children of believing parents (1 Cor 7:14), and the history of how the apostles carried out the Great Commission, which favors the conclusion, "that they admitted the children of believers along with their parents, and because of their relation to their parents, into the communion of the church by baptism."[21]

Cunningham observes that:

Men have often striven hard in their speculations to lay down something precise and definite, in the way of general principle or standard, as to the bearing and effect of baptism in relation to the great blessings of justification and regeneration in the case of infants individually. But Scripture really affords no adequate materials for doing this; for we have no warrant for asserting even in regards to infants, to whom it is God's purpose to give at some time justification and regeneration, that He uniformly or ordinarily gives it to them before or at their baptism. The discomfort of this state of uncertainty, the difficulty of laying down any definite doctrine upon this subject, has often led men to adopt one or other of two opposite extremes, which have the appearance of greater simplicity

---

20. Cunningham, "Zwingli and the Sacraments," 245–46.

21. Cunningham, *Historical Theology*, 2:149.

and definiteness—that is, either to deny the lawfulness
of infant baptism altogether, or to embrace the doctrine
of baptismal regeneration and to represent all baptized
infants, or at least all the baptized infants of believing
parents, as receiving these great blessings in and with
the external ordinance, or as certainly and infallibly to
receive them at some future time. But this is manifestly
unreasonable.[22]

Cunningham did not go into any great detail regarding the
arguments for and against infant baptism. He believed that the line
of argument to which he alluded, "though in some measure infer-
ential," was sufficient *in cumulo* to establish the conclusion "that the
children of believing parents are to be baptized."[23] He did, however,
seek to counter those who hold that "it is inconsistent with the
nature of baptism, as set before us in Scripture, that it should be
administered to any, except upon the ground of a previous possession of faith by the person receiving it."[24]

According to Cunningham, justification and regeneration
(the washing away of guilt, and the washing away of depravity), and
these alone, are

the spiritual blessings which the washing with water
in the name of the Father, and the Son, and the Holy
Ghost, directly signifies and represents. Faith does not
stand in the same relation to baptism as these blessings
do, and for this obvious and conclusive reason, that it is
not directly and expressly signified or represented in the
external ordinance itself, as they are.[25]

Faith, says Cunningham, is the ordinary means by which
those capable of it receive the blessings of justification and regeneration. However:

It is universally admitted that infants, though incapable
of faith, are capable of salvation, and are actually saved;

---

22. Cunningham, *Historical Theology*, 2:150–51.

23. Cunningham, *Historical Theology*, 2:149.

24. Cunningham, *Historical Theology*, 2:151.

25. Cunningham, *Historical Theology*, 2:152.

and they cannot be saved unless they be justified and regenerated. And since it is thus certain that infants actually receive the very blessings which baptism signifies and represents, without the presence of the faith which is necessary to the possession of these blessings in adults . . . there can be no serious difficulty in the idea of their admissibility to the outward sign and seal of these blessings, without a previous profession of faith.[26]

Baptism, it should be said, also represents union with Christ (which Cunningham recognizes elsewhere) and the baptism of the Spirit; or more properly, the blessings of justification and regeneration that result from union with Christ and the baptism of the Spirit. Cunningham regularly mentions only justification and regeneration, in that order, stating that they must both be received by faith in the case of adults. This is curious for a Reformed theologian, since Reformed theology generally teaches that regeneration precedes both faith and justification. It could be that Cunningham is using "regeneration" in the broader sense Calvin and some others did to represent the entire process of spiritual renewal.[27]

Returning to the earlier discussion of "Zwingli and the Doctrine of the Sacraments," Cunningham continues to develop his argument by examining statements in the Westminster Confession of Faith and the Larger Catechism. He also references numerous Reformed authorities whom he claims are in general agreement with him. He observes that those who "have not attended to and estimated aright this topic of the peculiar and subordinate place held by the subject of infant baptism are very apt to run into one or other of two extremes." These are that of "lowering the true sacramental principle, as brought out in the general definition of a sacrament, and as exhibited fully in the case of adult baptism and the Lord's Supper, to the level of what suits the special case of infant baptism," or that of "raising the explanation propounded of the bearing and effect of infant baptism, up to a measure of clearness and fulness which really attaches only to adult baptism and the Lord's Supper."[28]

---

26. Cunningham, *Historical Theology*, 2:152.

27. See e.g., Calvin, *Institutes*, 3.3.21.

28. Cunningham, "Zwingli and the Sacraments," 253.

Cunningham was insistent that no sharp distinction should be made between the qualifications for baptism and the Lord's Supper. In this, he was opposing the view discussed earlier, common in the Scottish Highlands and championed by its most noted minister John Kennedy, that made a distinction between members in full communion and those who were merely baptized adherents. (A similar position was expressed in the "Half-Way Covenant" in New England in the seventeenth century). As Kennedy noted (and defended), "The result of carrying this view into practice is well known; the numbers (*sic*) of members in full communion is comparatively small, and parents who have never communicated, receive baptism for their children."[29]

This debate was not central to Cunningham's view of baptism, but it is mentioned here because, in coming to sum up his argument, one of the points he makes is that baptism should only be administered to believers and their children, and those who receive baptism for their children should also be qualified to sit at the Lord's Table. This is the second of three points. The first is that "Scripture, while furnishing sufficient materials to establish the lawfulness and obligation of infant baptism, does not give us much direct information concerning it," and therefore "men should be particularly careful to abstain from deductions, probabilities or conjectures, beyond what Scripture clearly sanctions." The third point is that:

> while believers are warranted to improve the baptism of their children . . . neither parents nor children should regard the fact that they have been baptized, as affording of itself even the slightest presumption that they have been regenerated [without] the appropriate proofs of an actual renovation of the moral nature, exhibited in each case individually; and that, until such proof appear, every one, whether baptized or not, should be treated and dealt with in all respects as if he were unregenerate, and still needed to be born again of the word of God through the belief of the truth.[30]

---

29. Kennedy, *Days of the Fathers*, 125.

30. Cunningham, "Zwingli and the Sacraments," 290–91.

SUPPORT FOR CUNNINGHAM

As noted, Cunningham cites several sources he claims are in agreement with him. For instance, he quotes Martin Vitringa[31] at some length to the effect that "the sacraments have been instituted only for those who have received the grace of God."[32] Vitringa "gives extracts from eight to ten of the confessions of the Reformed period, and from above fifty of the most eminent divines of that and the succeeding century." The names of forty-nine (not "above fifty") divines are then listed, to which Cunningham adds, "in short, all the greatest divines of the sixteenth and seventeenth centuries."[33]

It is questionable whether all of the authorities cited by Cunningham would have agreed with him on the narrower point that adult baptism is the primary mode both biblically and confessionally. However, on the argument that the Westminster divines had adult baptism in mind when formulating their definition of the sacrament, Cunningham offers the names of fellow Scots Samuel Rutherford (1600–61), in his *Due Right of Presbyteries,* and George Gillespie (1613–48), in *Aaron's Rod Blossoming.* Rutherford and Gillespie are both quoted at length and Cunningham offers the opinion that

> Rutherford and Gillespie are, literally and without any exception, just the two very highest authorities that could be brought to bear upon a question of this kind, at once from their learning and ability as theologians, and from the place they held and the influence they exerted in the actual preparation of the documents under consideration.[34]

Cunningham continues,

---

31 Martin Vitringa was a nephew of the elder Campegius Vitringa (1643–1723) and a cousin of the younger Campegius Vitringa (1693–1731). Martin Vitringa edited the sixth edition of one of his uncle's works, *Doctrina Christianae Religionis,* published from 1761–76. See William Orme, *Bibliotheca Biblica,* 450. Martin Vitringa's exact dates could not be found.

32. Cunningham, "Zwingli and the Sacraments," 264–65.

33. Cunningham, "Zwingli and the Sacraments," 266.

34. Cunningham, "Zwingli and the Sacraments," 279.

> We think it of some importance to show, that these views
> of the sacramental principle, or of the doctrines of the
> sacraments, which though so clearly and fully set forth in
> the Westminster standards, have been so much lost sight
> of amongst us, were openly maintained by the leading
> divines of the Church of Scotland during last century.[35]

The names of Principal (James) Hadow (1667–1747) and Thomas
Boston (1678–1732) who "may be regarded as the heads of two
different schools of theology in Scotland in the early part of last
century,"[36] are offered as in agreement on the point in question.
Then there is a quotation from Dr. John Erskine (1721–1803),
"probably the greatest divine in the Church of Scotland in the latter
part of last century."[37]

The various divines Cunningham quotes or refers to all lived
before his time. His contemporary, James Bannerman, who was one
of two editors of Cunningham's posthumously published works, also
expressed himself much to the same effect, as quoted earlier.[38] One
who lived later into the twentieth century was another noted Scottish theologian, John Macleod (1872–1948), one-time principal of
the Free Church College, Edinburgh (1929–43). Towards the end of
his *Scottish Theology* (a series of lectures delivered at Westminster
Seminary in Philadelphia), he deals with developments subsequent
to Cunningham's time and notes how the High Church party in the
Church of Scotland advocated baptismal regeneration and "sought
to make out that the Reformed standards teach a doctrine of baptismal grace which issues in the actual regeneration of the baptised
through the sacrament as an instrument."[39] In response, Macleod
states that they did this

> oblivious of the two-fold fact that the statements of those
> standards deal primarily with what baptism is in the
> normal instance of its administration, that is, in the case

---

35. Cunningham, "Zwingli and the Sacraments," 281.

36. Cunningham, "Zwingli and the Sacraments," 281–82.

37. Cunningham, "Zwingli and the Sacraments," 283.

38. Bannerman, *Church of Christ* 2:108–09.

39. Macleod, *Scottish Theology,* 303.

of believers who are baptised on their own profession; and that the baptism of children as members of Christian households, though thoroughly warranted on its own grounds, is not the normal and regulative example of the administration of the sacrament.[40]

Whether directly influenced by Cunningham or not, there could be no clearer evidence of the continuing influence of the position he had advocated.

CRITICISMS OF CUNNINGHAM

Cunningham could point to fellow Scots in the past as supporting his view, also agreed to by his contemporary Bannerman, and John Macleod represented the same view in the early part of the twentieth century. However, another noted twentieth-century Scot, John Murray (1898–1975) disagreed. Murray did not speculate as to what was in the minds of the Westminster divines when they formulated their several definitions of baptism, but in a footnote in his *Christian Baptism*, he notes,

> William Cunningham and James Bannerman . . . maintained that a line of discrimination must be drawn between the baptism of infants and the baptism of adults. . . . It may be quite correct to say with Cunningham that adult baptism is "*that* from which mainly and principally we should form our conception of what baptism is and means and was intended to accomplish." But when Cunningham says that "it is adult baptism alone which embodies and brings out the full idea of the ordinance" . . . there does not appear to be good warrant for such discrimination.[41]

---

40. Macleod, *Scottish Theology*, 303–4.

41. Murray, *Christian Baptism*, 85n45 (italics original). For a view the exact opposite to that of Cunningham, see the Church of Scotland's 1958 *Interim Report*, which claims that for the Scottish Reformers "baptism by its very nature as the sacrament of our first entrance into God's household was essentially relevant for children but therefore equally adaptable to adults, who can only enter into the kingdom of God as little children" (12).

Murray makes his own view clear when he states positively that "Baptism has one import, and it bears that same import whether it is dispensed to adults or infants."[42] It should be administered, however, not on the basis of any assumptions about the spiritual state of the child, but simply because it is a divinely mandated ordinance. "Short of that we may not stop. Beyond that we may not go." At the same time, Murray goes on to state that "Baptized infants are to be received as children of God and treated accordingly."[43] Elsewhere, Murray commends Cunningham for "ably and cogently"[44] opposing the idea that "there is such a thing in the New Testament as dual confession, one entitling to baptism and another, of a higher order, entitling to communicant membership."[45]

A contemporary Scot, Sinclair Ferguson, in *John Owen on the Christian Life,* notes that "It is significant that [Owen's] definition [of baptism] is serviceable both for the baptism of adults upon profession of faith, and of infants of believing parents—a matter of some importance that was on occasion forgotten in the later development of the doctrine of baptism within the tradition of Owen's theology." Then in a footnote, Ferguson cites both Cunningham and Bannerman, as examples of those who "forgot." Of Cunningham's claim that it is "quite plain to anyone capable of reflecting on the subject, that it is adult baptism alone which brings out the full idea of the ordinance," Ferguson comments that "It was not obvious, it appears, to Owen. He does not seem to have adopted this dichotomy."[46]

Robert (Bob) Letham, a quintessential Englishman with partially Scottish roots, offers a trenchant critique of Cunningham in the context of a review of *The People's Theologian: Writings in Honour of Donald Macleod.* This book contains a number of essays on different subjects and Letham's review touches on them all, but a disproportionate amount of space is devoted to Michael W.

---

42. Murray, *Christian Baptism*, 86.

43. Murray, *Christian Baptism*, 55–56.

44. Murray, *Christian Baptism*, 80n42.

45. Murray, *Christian Baptism*, 80.

46. Ferguson, *John Owen on the Christian Life*, 215.

Honeycutt's contribution: "William Cunningham and the Doctrine of the Sacraments." Letham charges Cunningham's baptismal theology with being hardly distinguishable from a credobaptist one. Cunningham was, in Letham's view "wrong; totally, monumentally wrong." He continues:

> It is true that Cunningham did not have access to the full minutes of the Assembly, which have only recently been transcribed. . . . Moreover, Cunningham's primary appeal is to the *Shorter Catechism,* from which detailed theological statement was expressly excluded.
>
> There were a range of discussions on baptism at the Assembly, more fully-recorded by the scribe than most other matters. These covered both the theology and practice of baptism. In each case, the baptism of *infants* was in view. There is no evidence that the divines considered this in isolation from the baptism of adult converts. . . .
>
> Moreover, the *Directory for the Publick Worship of God* refers to 'the child to be baptised'. The words of instruction before baptism speak of the reasons why 'the seed and posterity of the faithful, born within the church' have interest in the covenant and the right to its seal.[47]

Scarcely less severe is the critique of the late David F. Wright. From 1984 until his death, Wright wrote a number of essays on baptism, twenty-seven of which, in 2007, were published together in *Infant Baptism in Historical Perspective: Collected Studies.* Wright wrote an introduction to this book: "The Strange History of Infant Baptism, Not Least in Scotland." Coming to William Cunningham and his essay on "Zwingli and the Doctrine of the Sacraments," Wright found it to abound in "insightful one-sidedness . . . driven

---

47. Letham, "Book Review," 75–76 (italics original). Letham also makes the point that Rutherford and Gillespie, while involved in debates at the Westminster Assembly, were nonvoting Scottish commissioners. In an October 9, 2019 email, he says that Cunningham's "summary of the Protestant doctrine of the sacraments is amazing for its inaccuracy." A one-time Reformed Baptist, Letham is the author of *The Water That Unites*, where his paedobaptist convictions are developed in a more positive and irenic manner.

by the bogeyman of baptismal regeneration."[48] Wright independently came to the view, based on historical research into early church sources, as well as the "increasingly widespread" consensus among New Testament scholars,[49] that believers' baptism was the New Testament norm and so found Cunningham's analysis on that point "sound in its fundamental instinct," but failing "to recognize that it indicts most Protestant theology from the reformers on and that the genius of the Westminster divines was indeed to start with the baptism of believers but not leave infant baptism out in unilluminated darkness."[50] Cunningham's interpretation of the Westminster Confession and Catechisms was "bizarre." He did not "set out to work with scripture" and was "no more than selective in his engagement with the actual Westminster documents."[51]

Wright is only slightly less critical of Bannerman, whom he finds to be "more balanced and rounded" than Cunningham. He does consider Cunningham and Bannerman to have been right insofar as believers' baptism "is in an appropriate sense the norm of Christian baptism. They were ahead of their time, but they spoiled their case by exaggeration, and by bifurcating the baptismal waters like the Red Sea at the exodus."[52] Wright says that he now understands "with fresh clarity" how "evangelical circles in my adoptive land which still set such store by the Westminster Confession come to profess such a base estimate of baptism."[53]

If William Cunningham did not have access to the minutes of the Westminster Assembly, David Wright did. It is on this basis

---

48. Wright, *Infant Baptism*, xxxvi.

49. Wright, *Infant Baptism*, 5. Wright also discusses the 1982 report of the Faith and Order Commission of the World Council of Churches in which representatives of various traditions from Baptist to Roman Catholic agreed that, "While the possibility that infant baptism was also practiced in the apostolic age cannot be excluded, baptism upon personal profession of faith is the most clearly attested pattern in the New Testament documents" (Wright, *Infant Baptism*, 312).

50. Wright. *Infant Baptism*, xxxvii.

51. Wright, *Infant Baptism*, xxxvi.

52. Wright, *Infant Baptism*, xl.

53. Wright, *Infant Baptism*, x–xl.

that he delivered a public lecture on "Baptism at the Westminster Assembly," at a conference commemorating that Assembly.[54] Among other things, such as public-versus-private baptisms, the debate over dipping (immersion as an alternative to sprinkling), and the meaning of federal holiness in 1 Corinthians 7:14, Wright argued that the Westminster divines intended the documents they produced to be understood in a "realist sense," and so to teach baptismal regeneration, and this is what was meant by the Confession of Faith's calling baptism "the instrument and occasion of regeneration by the Spirit, of the remission of sins, of ingrafting into Christ (cf. 28:1)."[55] This is an understanding Cunningham would have vigorously opposed. He believed it to be a "most extraordinary blunder" to hold that the early Protestant confessions, both during the Reformation and in the seventeenth century, taught baptismal regeneration.[56] However, it seems clear that he and Wright were using the term in two different ways. Cunningham meant by it the *ex opere operato* approach of Rome, whereas Wright meant it in a more qualified sense. Letham explains it in this way:

> The Reformed construal of baptismal regeneration is very different [from the Roman Catholic one] for obvious reasons. It is based on the fact that both baptism and regeneration mark the start of the Christian life. Regeneration/resurrection/renewal in this sense are effectively stating the same thing—union with Christ in his death and resurrection, to which baptism is integrally related, as per Rom 6, Titus 3 *et al*. . . . So there is a *theological* connection between baptism and regeneration. It is *not causal*—unlike Rome baptism is not the efficient cause of regeneration. It has *no necessary temporal connection*. Baptism follows faith or precedes faith in the NT, and for all we know may be simultaneous. The time of regeneration is completely unknown to us. The relation

---

54. Wright, *Infant Baptism*, 238–56.

55. Wright, *Infant Baptism*, 244.

56. Cunningham, "Zwingli and the Sacraments," 241.

is *theological*—and is to be understood in the wider context of election and faith (as the WCF does).[57]

Likewise, Wright acknowledges that the Confession of Faith offers a "variety of qualifications" to the assertion that "the grace promised is not only offered, but really exhibited and conferred by the Holy Ghost (28:6)." Efficacy "is not tied to the moment of administration (28:6), grace and salvation are not so inseparably annexed to baptism that no person can be regenerated or saved without it (28:5) or that all baptized are undoubtedly regenerated (28:5)." Regeneration "is not automatically enjoyed by all recipients: it contains 'a promise of benefit to worthy receivers' (27:3), who from one point of view are 'those who actually profess faith in and obedience unto Christ, but also the infants of one or both believing parents (28:4)' and from another 'such (whether of age or infants) as that grace belongeth unto, according to the counsel of God's own will, in his appointed time (28:6).'"[58]

At the same time, while highly critical of Cunningham's interpretation of the Westminster standards and of the doctrine of baptism in general, Wright (unlike Letham) does agree with Cunningham (although for different reasons) that believers' (although not necessarily adult) baptism was the biblical and Christian norm.

OBSERVATIONS

So where does this leave us? First, in response to Letham's charge that Cunningham's primary appeal was to the Shorter Catechism; this may be true, but he also made repeated references to the Larger Catechism and the Confession of Faith. To quote just one of many:

> The Larger Catechism agrees with the Confession of Faith and the Shorter Catechism, in setting forth this great doctrine in regard to the subjects of the sacraments, viz. that they are intended for believers, for those who already have the gift of faith; not meaning to exclude the baptism of infants—which was regarded as fully sanctioned by

57. Letham, email April 12, 2021 (italics original).
58. Wright, *Infant Baptism*, 244–45.

scriptural authority—but virtually conceding, 1st, That the full and adequate idea of a sacrament, as exhibited in adult baptism and the Lord's Supper, does not directly and thoroughly apply to the case of infant baptism; and 2d, That it is of more importance to bring out fully and explicitly, the sacramental principle, the true and full doctrine of the sacraments—as applicable to adult baptism and the Lord's Supper, than to attempt to lay down some more vague and diluted view upon this subject, which might include the special and peculiar case of the baptism of infants.[59]

It is, however, admittedly difficult to see how the Westminster divines were thinking primarily of adult baptism in their various definitions. In the Shorter Catechism, for instance, they move directly from their definition of baptism to say that it is "not to be administered to any that are out of the visible church, till they profess their faith in Christ, and obedience to him; but the infants of such as are members of the visible church are to be baptized" (A 95). This seems to imply infant baptism being at least as normative as adult baptism, if not more so. The Larger Catechism (Q&A 166) says much the same. The Confession of Faith's definition of baptism (28:1) does give the appearance (even more so perhaps than those of the catechisms), of being most applicable to believers; yet then we are told, as referenced by Wright above, that it is not only for those who actually profess faith, but for their infants (28:4) and, further, the grace promised is ". . . to such (whether of age or infants) as that grace belongeth unto, according to the counsel of God's own will, in His appointed time" (28:6). There is no suggestion of infant baptism having a subordinate place to adult baptism, although equally clearly the grace of baptism is not tied to the moment of administration.

It does appear that Cunningham was reading his own view back into the Westminster standards, but does that make him wrong in light of "the lamp of divine truth?"[60] Clearly, he was opposed to any suggestion of baptismal regeneration, which he

---

59. Cunningham, "Zwingli and the Sacraments," 275–76.

60. Campbell and Maclean, *People's Theologian*, 110.

understood in terms of water baptism having an intrinsic power to effect justification and regeneration. Wright defined baptismal regeneration differently, with several qualifications, and insisted that this is what the Westminster divines meant by describing baptism as "the instrument and occasion of regeneration by the Spirit, of the remission of sins, of ingrafting into Christ (WCF 28:1)."[61]

Wright says that the Westminster definition of baptism was a "realist" one and this implies baptismal regeneration in the sense explained above. Nevertheless, I find his use of "baptismal regeneration" (for all its qualifications) unhelpful. A clearer understanding of what is meant by "realist" is offered by Jack Collins in a two-part essay, "What Does Baptism Do for Anyone?" According to Collins, "The Christian tradition, from its earliest stages, has held to some kind of 'baptismal realism,' that is the view that by means of baptism God actually effects some change in the condition of the person baptized."[62] But what is the nature of that change? Drawing on the "sacramental realism" of the Levitical system in which a person, animal or object becomes either ritually clean or unclean, Collins argues that this ritual or "administrative" cleanness carries over into the New Testament doctrine of baptism. "In the biblical worldview the cleansing ceremony effects a change in one's administrative status—a change that should be accompanied by moral vitality. . ." Thus, Paul addresses believers and their children as "saints," then urges them to live as such (e.g., Eph 1:1; 6:1–4). Further, by a study of three New Testament expressions for "regeneration" or "being born again," Collins suggests "There is no reason why all these terms must refer to exactly the same thing, nor is it entirely clear that they correspond to what has now become the meaning of 'regeneration/new birth.'"[63] He argues that a "new birth" in the "ritual or administrative sense" fits the usage of two of the terms used in the New Testament (Titus 3:5; 1 Pet 1:3, 23). Paul's use of "union with Christ" language is explained in the same way. We need to realize that Paul (and other New Testament writers,

---

61. Wright, *Infant Baptism*, 244. It does appear that at least some of the West-minster divines used the language of baptismal regeneration in a positive sense.

62. Collins, "What Does Baptism Do?," 1.

63. Collins, "What Does Baptism Do?," 86–87.

such as Peter and the author of Hebrews) "did not generally speak the way a Reformed systematician would. Rather, according to Paul's normal usage, to be a baptized member of the people of God is to enjoy familial privileges and spiritual influences . . . advantages that oblige us to respond with living and lifelong faith."[64]

On the meaning of regeneration:

> In order to discuss the relationship of baptism to "regeneration," we need to clarify which sense of "regeneration" we have in view. If we mean it in the ritual or administrative sense, i.e., entry into a new life as a member of the people of God, there is no conceptual or theological difficulty with saying baptism brings about "regeneration." . . . If we mean regeneration in the narrower sense, i.e., as the result of effectual calling, then the only affirmation possible is that it is in God's hands: further than that we cannot go.[65]

A great deal of confusion has arisen in recent years, especially as a result of the so-called "Federal Vision" and its use of "baptismal regeneration" in what Collins calls the "administrative" or "ritual" sense, which Federal Vision advocates prefer to call its "objective" sense. A representative of this movement, Rick Lusk, has written about this in "Do I Believe in Baptismal Regeneration?" He wisely says that he seldom uses the term because of the confusion it causes, but then proceeds to defend its "objective" use both from Scripture and church history, noting that following the Synod of Dordt (1618–19) "the meaning of the term 'regeneration' narrowed to the moment of God's initiating grace in a person's life, resulting in life-long faith and repentance. It becomes almost exclusively subjective and individual, rather than corporate and cosmic."[66] Lusk rejects baptismal regeneration in this subjective sense, but affirms it in the objective sense of representing the fact that one is outwardly a member of the Christian church, God's new covenant community. Since we humans are incapable of reading one another's hearts, we

---

64. Collins, "What Does Baptism Do?," 25.

65. Collins, "What Does Baptism Do?," 89.

66. Lusk, "Do I Believe in Baptismal Regeneration?," para. 20.

can only deal with one another in terms of objective reality. Lusk may very well be accurate both biblically and historically, but this objective/subjective distinction has not been clearly understood or as carefully explained as by Lusk.[67]

In my view, a more helpful approach is made by Tony Lane and others (with slight variations) to the effect that repentance, faith, baptism, and the reception of the Holy Spirit all belong together in the New Testament understanding of receiving salvation. Thus, those passages that appear to give to the act of baptism a redemptive or regenerating significance are to be understood in the context of the whole. The various other elements are present as well.[68] This is similar to what the Confession of Faith means when it says of sacraments in general, "There is in every sacrament a spiritual relation, or sacramental union, between the sign and the thing signified: whence it comes to pass, that the names and effects of the one are attributed to the other."[69] It also implies believers' baptism as being the biblical norm, which Cunningham maintained and Wright also recognized.

Cunningham refers consistently to *adult* rather than *believers'* baptism. Believers' baptism in established churches need not be of adults only, but the concept of missionary baptism implies that it is of adult heads of families who then bring their families into the church with them as members of a believing family. These would normally be the fathers of the respective families, although the case of Lydia (Acts 16:15) shows that this is not necessarily always the case. Whether or not infants were present in the household baptisms of the New Testament is not the issue so much as on what basis members of the household were baptized—was it their own

---

67. Elsewhere, Lusk describes the Federal Vision outlook at "catholic" rather than "sectarian," stating that it "would like to learn from other traditions within Christendom, trusting that God will continue to bring his church to greater confessional maturity in the time to come" ("From Birmingham with Love," 154). To date, it has largely been a cause of division within Reformed circles, with, no doubt, fault on all sides.

68. Wright, *Baptism*, 144. Cf. Beasley-Murray, *Baptism in the New Testament*, 263–305; Dunn, *Baptism in the Holy Spirit*, 91; Stein, in Schreiner and Wright, *Believer's Baptism*, 35–66.

69. *Westminster Confession of Faith*, 27.2.

profession or that of the head of the household? What then of children growing up in Christian families, which is the norm in both Baptist and paedobaptist churches today? These questions are addressed later.

Meanwhile, Cunningham's view (and that of others cited in support) represents an honorable position in Scottish theology and qualifies for what Ken Stewart urges as "this more modest place"[70] for infant baptism. This despite the fact that it represents a departure from the Reformation-era *Forme of Prayers*, often known as Knox's liturgy, received by the Church of Scotland in 1564, which "took no cognisance of other than infant baptism."[71]

---

70. Stewart, *In Search of Ancient Roots*, 139.

71. Wright, *Infant Baptism*, 236. The same was true of the English *Book of Common Prayer* "until shortly before [it was changed in] the 1662 revision, and then only grudgingly."

4

Present-Day Implications
for Missionary Baptism

IT SEEMS TO ME that if we are to attribute the same significance to infant baptism as to believers' baptism, the most logical approach is that of presumptive election (as in Hodge) or presumptive regeneration (as in Kuyper). This study argues instead that a view closer to Cunningham's will help clear up misunderstandings between fellow-believers, and further, that a dual practice of infant baptism and baby dedication will promote the unity of Christ's church. I arrive at this conclusion by a consideration of the following evidence.

THE CIRCUMCISION/BAPTISM ANALOGY

There are Baptists who would agree with Letham's assessment of Cunningham,[1] while finding his argument for infant baptism unconvincing. As noted in the previous chapter, this argument (brief as it is) follows traditional lines of covenant continuity and federal holiness. However, Cunningham makes no explicit mention of what lies at the heart of the covenant continuity argument, the circumcision/baptism analogy (Gen 17; Col 2:10). This seems curious, especially as Huldrych Zwingli, the subject

---

1. See Puritan Board, "William Cunningham on Baptism."

of Cunningham's essay, "Zwingli and the Sacraments," is credited with having developed this argument that became a staple of the Reformed defense of infant baptism.[2]

An original approach to the circumcision/baptism analogy is offered by Meredith Kline (1922–2007) in *By Oath Consigned*, based on his research into extrabiblical suzerainty treaties. Kline sees circumcision and baptism as involving both malediction and consecration, covenant curse as well as covenant blessing. There are some difficulties with this approach, not least that Scripture nowhere speaks of circumcision and baptism in this way, although as Kline points out, it does speak metaphorically of "a baptism of fire" (Luke 12:50; cf. Matt 3:11).[3] The argument depends on reading extrabiblical examples into the biblical text. For instance, in stating that baptism is a form of water ordeal, Kline appeals for support of this concept to Qumranic and Ugaritic texts, while also referencing Israel's Red Sea ordeal and the Noahic deluge (1 Cor 12:2; 1 Pet 3:21), as well as Israel's passing through the Jordan River to inherit the land of Canaan.[4] However, debatable as Kline's approach may be, it is a reminder that all biblical covenants have two sides, blessings to those who obey and curses on those who disobey. To quote Sinclair Ferguson:

> The redemptive covenants of Scripture all have this struc-
> ture. Given to people already under the curse, they offer
> the blessing of salvation to those who trust and obey. If
> people spurn the covenant in unbelief and disobedience,
> the curse remains. This is the pattern with Noah (Gen
> 5:29; 6:13; 8:21), with Abraham (Gen 15:7–21) and also
> with Moses (Ex 6: 2–8; 34: 10–18; Deut 28–30). The pat-
> tern finds its ultimate fulfillment in Christ. He enters

2. Cottrell, "Zwingli's Covenant Theology." Cottrell notes the influence of Augustine's theology, but fails to mention his use of the circumcision/baptism analogy, although he does recognize that Zwingli's use of the analogy was not new. (According to Wright, the use of the analogy was discussed in the time of Cyprian at a council of African bishops in 253. See *Infant Baptism*, 29–31.)

3. Collins notes tersely, "The argument of Meredith Kline . . . being . . . methodologically unsound, will receive no further interaction here" ("What Does Baptism Do?," 13n24).

4. Kline, *By Oath Consigned*, 55–62.

into humanity's accursed situation and bears the divine anathema so that the blessing promised to Abraham might come to the Gentiles (Gal 3:13–14; cf. the cry of dereliction Mk 15:34).[5]

In general, Baptists have rejected the circumcision/baptism analogy, as did Karl Barth (1886–1986), the father of neo-orthodoxy (a moniker he did not use), at least in the way it has been traditionally applied. In *The Teaching of the Church Regarding Baptism*, Barth dismissed circumcision as belonging to the nation of Israel and charged infant baptism with being linked to the "Constantinian" state-church concept in Europe.[6] In his commentary on the Heidelberg Catechism, he clarifies that "It is correct that baptism replaces circumcision," but goes on to say:

> Is not that which distinguished Israel from other nations (the distinction symbolized by circumcision) the fact that from this nation the *One* should come? And is not the history of this nation ended after that was fulfilled and he has come? Are not Israel and the church two different things, and is one not accepted into the community of the new covenant on the basis of *faith*? . . . The church is no longer Israel, and Israel was not yet the church, although it is true that the covenant of God has this double form. But this means that the argument for infant baptism is not valid. We can only say that in both cases we are dealing with signs of the covenant, but signs of a different kind."[7]

---

5. Wright, *Baptism*, 98.

6. "Circumcision refers to natural birth; it is the sign of the election of the holy lineage of Israel, which with the birth of the Messiah achieved its goal, so that therewith this sign lost its meaning" (Barth, *Teaching of the Church Regarding Baptism*, 43–44). "Am I wrong in thinking that the really operative extraneous ground for infant-baptism, even with the Reformers, and ever again quite plainly since, has been this: one did not want then in any case or at any price to deny the existence of the evangelical Church in the Constantinian *corpus christianum*—and today one does not want to renounce the present form of the national church (*Volkskirche*)?" (52–54).

7. Barth, *Learning Jesus through the Heidelberg Catechism*, 103–4 (italics original). Based on lectures published in 1948 and 1960. In what proved to be his final word on the subject several years later, Barth did recognize the force

Paul Jewett (1919–91) saw Barth as anticipating his own argument in *Infant Baptism and the Covenant of Grace*.[8] Jewett nevertheless acknowledges that Old Testament circumcision also "becomes a symbol of renewal and cleansing of heart" (Deut 10:16; Jer 4:4; Rom 2:29), and in discussing Colossians 2:11–13 he states,

> to experience the circumcision of Christ in the putting off of the body of the flesh, is the same as being buried with him and being raised with him through faith. If this be true, the only conclusion we can reach is that the two signs, as outward rites, symbolize the same inner reality in Paul's thinking. Thus circumcision may fairly be said to be the Old Testament counterpart to baptism.[9]

An earlier monogram by Jewett, *Infant Baptism and Confirmation*, provided a scholarly basis for David Kingdon's 1973 book, *Children of Abraham*, in which he states regarding circumcision/ baptism,

> The analogy does in fact exist, but it is the nature of it which is in question. The covenant with Abraham included promises that his physical seed would be multiplied and given a land. In the New Testament this is seen as a spiritual seed and a spiritual inheritance. . . . The abrogation of the principle "thee and thy seed" is seen in the New Covenant (Jer. 31:31–34) where possession of inward spiritual life is required.[10]

Kingdon's popular work represents a resurgence of Reformed Baptist thinking that accepts the unity (as well as the diversity) of the old and new covenants and claims to be in continuity with the

---

of Calvin's use of the analogy, but not without qualification. See Barth, *Church Dogmatics*, 4:195–96. In this later work, he says that his *Baptism* book was "outdated from my own standpoint" (ix).

8. Jewett, *Infant Baptism and the Covenant of Grace*, 92.

9. Jewett, *Infant Baptism and the Covenant of Grace*, 86, 89.

10. Kingdon, *Children of Abraham*, 6. Wright alludes to the assertion in the Epistle of Barnabas that the counterpart of circumcision in the flesh is circumcision of the ears and heart by the Holy Spirit (Barn. 9:1–9; 10:11) but it was not associated with baptism (Wright, *Infant Baptism*, 53).

Second London Baptist Confession of 1689.[11] In recent years, there have been a plethora of similar publications, among the most helpful of which are collections of essays in *Believer's Baptism* (edited by Thomas Schreiner and Shawn Wright) and *Recovering a Covenantal Heritage* (edited by Richard Barcellos). The point being made is that in the heightened spirituality of the new covenant, it is those circumcised in heart (i.e., the regenerate) who are the true children of Abraham (Gal 3:26–28, etc.).

HOUSEHOLD/MISSIONARY BAPTISM

Paedobaptists regularly point out that the difficulty with this line of reasoning is that it is humanly impossible to guarantee the regenerate church membership claimed by Baptists as the New Testament norm.[12] There are examples of professed believers falling away (Acts 8:18–24; 1 Tim 1:20), as well as warnings about that possibility (John 15: 2, 6; Rom 11:13–21; Heb 6:4–6; 9:13–20). What the New Testament pattern indicates is the missionary baptism of professed believers. It is possible to acknowledge this, while still affirming that the model of some half of ten missionary baptisms mentioned in the New Testament is of converts *and their households* (even granting that in at least some cases, all members of the household believed).[13] This recalls Cunningham's point that if paedobaptists were more in the habit of witnessing adult baptism, as happens in missionary situations, they would have less difficulty understanding baptism's significance. Furthermore, Peter's reference to baptism includes Noah and his household (1 Pet 3:20–22) and Paul speaks of the entire people of Israel being baptized into Moses in

---

11. It was first published in 1688, but is generally referred to as the 1689 Confession. It is also known as the 1689 Baptist Confession of Faith. It was adopted in slightly modified form as the Philadelphia Confession of Faith.

12. See e.g., Strawbridge, *Case for Covenantal Infant Baptism*, 272–85. It was when he began to see that the new covenant includes warnings of apostasy (Heb 10:28–30) that Strawbridge's study of the issue "took a decisive turn" in his movement from a Reformed Baptist to a paedobaptist position (4).

13. On the other hand, Acts 8:12 refers to both men and women being baptized, with no mention of households or children.

the cloud and in the sea (1 Cor 10:2). Of the examples of baptism in the book of Acts, two were clearly of single men with no families of their own (Acts 4:36–38; 9:18, cf. 1 Cor 7:7 for confirmation of Paul's single status). Household baptism is generally a second line of reasoning in paedobaptist polemic, but I agree with Ken Stewart that it should be the primary one.[14]

The German scholar Joachim Jeremias did extensive research into what he called the "*oikos*-formula," from the Greek term for "household." He also researched the origins of proselyte baptism, whereby gentile converts to Judaism who were heads of households would be both circumcised and then baptized along with their families, although children born subsequently were not baptized. Jeremias first held this to be the case with Christian converts (i.e., children born subsequent to the parents' conversion were not baptized), but later changed his position.[15]

Jeremias's fellow countryman, Kurt Aland, replied to him, questioning his claims as to the antiquity of infant baptism. Aland devoted a chapter to the *oikos*-formula, arguing that

> the data that can be gathered from the New Testament seem to me in no way to justify the confidence with which the existence of infant baptism in New Testament times, or even quite generally of the baptism of children, is derived nowadays from the "*oikos*-formula." I would even contest whether we have any right to talk about an "*oikos*-formula" in the New Testament."[16]

Jeremias replied to Aland's reply, with *The Origins of Infant Baptism*, in which he states:

> The house in the narrower sense includes . . . the father of the family, the mother of the family and the children of every age; in the wider sense the relations living in

---

14. Stewart, *In Search of Ancient Roots*, 135.

15. Jeremias, *Infant Baptism in the First Four Centuries*, 43–58.

16. Aland, *Did the Early Church Baptize Infants?*, 91. Beasley-Murray offers an extended discussion of household baptisms in *Baptism in the New Testament*, 312–20. He also finds "no clear trace of influence" from proselyte baptism "on the interpretation of baptism in the New Testament" (330).

the house were also reckoned in, but not the servants without further comment. It is natural to conclude from this that the references to the "whole" household are intended in the first place to include the children. We do not assert that in each case children were, in fact, actually present. But we do mean that Paul and Luke could under no circumstances have used the phrase, "a household" or "his whole family" were baptized, if they had wished to say that only adults had been baptized.[17]

Kline takes "household" in a broader sense to include servants and suggest that "if it could be shown that servants were received into the church on the basis of the authority principle, it would follow *a fortiori* that the continuity with the Old Testament practice included infants too." He continues, "But what has to be determined is whether the household subordinates who were involved, of whatever variety, were received and baptized on the basis of personal conviction and confession or because they belonged to the household of the one who confessed the Christian faith." Then Kline concedes, "And that is where certainty does not appear attainable."[18]

Of the biblical examples of household baptisms, the one that provides the most support for a paedobaptist interpretation is of the Philippian jailer's baptism recorded in Acts 16:31–34. The NIV records that following his baptism, along with that of his household, "He was filled with joy because he had come to believe in God—he and his whole family" (Acts 16:34b). The ESV, on the other hand, has "And he rejoiced along with his entire household that he had believed in God," placing the emphasis on the fact that *he* believed, and *they* rejoiced along with him. This is closer to a literal translation than is the NIV. However, F. F. Bruce (1910–90), in his commentary on Acts, notes, "Here the adverb [*panoike*, 'with his entire household'] may be taken grammatically with either *ēgalliasato* ['he rejoiced'] or *pepisteukōs* ['he having believed']; in

---

17. Jeremias, *Origins of Infant Baptism*, 12.

18. Kline, *By Oath Consigned*, 97. On the related question of the baptism of infants born into Christian households, Wright observes that the evidence "will sustain the confidence of neither a Jeremias nor of an Aland" (*Infant Baptism*, 20.)

sense it probably goes with both."[19] Bruce Ware, in offering the Baptist perspective in *Baptism: Three Views*, notes that if Bruce is correct that the household phrase goes both with believing and rejoicing, "we have strong reason to dismiss the notion that the jailer's household included infants."[20] He continues,

> What makes the most sense here is that. . . (t)he offer of salvation is given to the jailer specifically while also including his house (Acts 16:31). Paul and Silas spoke the word of the Lord specifically to the jailer but included with him were all that were in the house (Acts 16:32). Then the jailer was baptized (single verb), he along with all his family (Acts 16:33). Finally, he rejoiced and believed in God, along with his entire household (Acts 16:34).[21]

In support of this interpretation, Ware points to a parallel situation in Acts 18:8 which states that "Crispus . . . believed. . . together with his entire household."[22]

On the other hand, James (Jim) W. Scott, referring to the Philippian jailer's household, notes:

> The key word in this passage is "with." It signifies accompaniment. When Luke says that the jailer heard the gospel and believed with his household, the implication is that everyone in his household went along with him. Any older household members, such as his wife, evidently became believers, too. But any young children went along with their father, following his lead with whatever limited understanding that they had.

---

19. Bruce, *Acts of the Apostles*, 365.

20. Wright, *Baptism*, 32.

21. Wright, *Baptism*, 32–33.

22. Wright, *Baptism*, 34. Not surprisingly, Ware also rejects the view that "the promise is for you and for your children" in Acts 2:39 is relevant to infant baptism. However, it is difficult to think that Jews hearing this for the first time, with their Old Testament covenantal background, would not have interpreted it in a paedobaptist fashion. See Beeke and Lanning in Strawbridge, *Case for Covenantal Infant Baptism*, 49–69. They quote Francis Schaeffer as saying Peter would have started a riot among his Jewish listeners, with their covenantal understanding, if he had excluded their children from baptism that day.

This crucial distinction between "with" and "and" (regrettably obscured by some translations) is clear in similar passages in Acts: 1:14; 3:4; 4:27; 5:1; 10:2; 14:13; 15:22; 21:5. In each case, "with" introduces those who follow the lead of others and join with them in their activity, however actively or passively. In Acts 21:5, for example, Paul is escorted to the harbor by all the men in the church at Tyre, "with wives and children," which no doubt included a number of small infants.

In the household baptism passages, the head of the house always believes "with" his household, but he and they are baptized. Just as the heads of households escorted Paul to the harbor "with" infants who were only passive participants, so also heads of households were baptized "with" whatever infants were in their families.[23]

These differing interpretations suggest to me the wisdom of Kline's concession (see above) that "certainty does not appear attainable" as to whether members of households in Acts were baptized on the basis of the head of the household's faith or their own. Likewise, J. I. Packer (1926–2020) notes that infant baptism is a practice that the New Testament "neither illustrates nor prescribes nor forbids."[24] David Wright urges his fellow paedobaptists "to abandon over-argued efforts to prove that infants were baptized in the churches of the New Testament. That in fact they were cannot (so I judge) be ruled out, but the case falls far short of proof, and advocates of baptizing babies are on safer territory in relying on biblical-theological rather than historical grounds."[25]

But surely, we can at least agree with Sinclair Ferguson when he says,

> God deals with families (Ps 68:6). . . . This is further exhibited in the way in which Paul's letters include children as "saints" and exhorts them to fulfill specifically covenantal responsibilities: "Obey your parents in the Lord for that is right (Eph 1:1, 6:1–3; cf. Col 1:2; 3:20)." Paul's

23. Scott, "Biblical Basis for Infant Baptism," paras. 31–33.

24. Packer, *Concise Theology*, 214.

25. Wright, *Infant Baptism*, 377.

appeal to the Mosaic covenant in the Ephesian context implies that the same dynamic which grounded the relationship of parents and children in the old continues in the new.[26]

Later, after quoting the Westminster Larger Catechism's answer to the question "How is our baptism to be improved?" (Q & A 167), and noting that the principles of Ephesians 6:1–4 "apply to every aspect of parental responsibility and children's experience," Ferguson adds:

> None of this should be misunderstood as implying that paedobaptists believe their children do not need to "be converted." True, many children from Christian families cannot remember a decisive "conversion" moment, but "conversion" should not be reduced to a moment of psychological crisis. It is simply shorthand for the faith and repentance which marks the continuance as well as the beginning of the Christian life. The gospel sign of baptism—whether received in infancy or in later years on profession of faith—calls us all to this lifelong conversion.[27]

David Wright provides postapostolic evidence from the *Apostolic Tradition* (c. 220 AD) of instructions for baptism that placed "the little children" first "with a distinction between those who can speak for themselves, who shall indeed do so, and those who cannot, for whom the parents or other family members will speak."[28] However, "It is not until the early years of the fifth century . . . that we encounter the first evidence of how parents or others did speak for the children." They were asked "Does he/she believe?" to which

---

26. Wright, *Baptism*, 106–7. See also Wilson, *To a Thousand Generations*, and Wilson, "Baptism and Children," 286–302.

27. Wright, *Baptism*, 110–11. Bonhoeffer suggests that "little children" in 1 John 2:12 should be taken literally along with "fathers" and "young men" in the ensuing verses. If so, this may be added to the "usual passages quoted as evidence for the practice of infant baptism in New Testament times" (*Cost of Discipleship*, 235n1).

28. Wright, *What Has Infant Baptism Done to Baptism?*, 39.

the reply was given "He/she believes."[29] Augustine explained this in terms of baptism being the sacrament of faith, such that "a child is made a believer (*fidelem*), though not yet by that faith (*fides*) which resides in the will of those believing, nevertheless already by the sacrament of that faith."[30]

Wright notes that "If one adopts the reading of the evidence given by Joachim Jeremias . . . then one must believe that in the early fifth century infant baptism was all but universal for the children of Christians." Yet Wright claims (contrary to Jeremias's later opinion) that there exists "a great deal of hard evidence in the fourth and early fifth centuries that the offspring of Christian parents . . . were not baptized as babies."[31] Household baptism was missionary baptism.

Cunningham believed that children "whether baptized or not, should be treated and dealt with in all respects as . . . unregenerate, still needing to be born again."[32] Kingdon expresses himself similarly: "Believers' children are privileged children because they are within the sphere of the preaching and nurture of the church, but they are not made Christian children by privilege, but by true conversion of the word of God through the belief of the truth."[33] This is the opposite of presumptive regeneration. A mediating position is offered by Dr. J. Douma, responding to both Kuyper and Kingdon that:

---

29. Wright, *What Has Infant Baptism Done to Baptism?*, 41–42. Cf. Hippolytus, *Apostolic Tradition*, 21:12–18; Bradshaw et al., *Apostolic Tradition*, 88–95.

30. Wright, *What Has Infant Baptism Done to Baptism?* 51. Wright references Keefe, *Water and the Word*, 2:349. He (Wright) comments, "This was hardly Augustine at his most impressive. . ."

31. Wright, *Infant Baptism*, 42–43.

32. Cunningham, "Zwingli and the Sacraments," 91.

33. Kingdon, *Children of Abraham*, 99. In a strongly worded critique of Kingdon's book, de Witt faults him with failing in one of his stated goals of developing a theology of children and of believers' children in particular. This promise "proves illusory in the end. The answer given is precisely that children, the children of believers, the 'children of Abraham,' are not so related" ("Children and the Covenant of Grace," 252).

our children are Christian children. By the call of God (and not their own "Christianity") they are separated from the children of this world. But they must accordingly behave as children of God. That does not come by itself; and *with* Kingdon we are against all false security. We heartily agree with him that one should not presume that our children are regenerate, for such a presumption cultivates that false security. . . . But it does not cultivate false security when we say, as opposed to Kingdon, "You are a Christian child," and then add with Kingdon, "Repent and believe the gospel." For conversion and faith are daily matters, a calling for our adults as well as our children.[34]

The Westminster Directory for Publick Worship of God states of children brought for the baptism that "they are Christians, and federally holy before baptism. . ."[35] Tony Lane, notes that in practice "even Baptists" who take their children to church and teach them to pray do not treat them as pagans, even though they are in need of personal conversion and commitment. He suggests that we may speak of Christian children in the same way as we talk of Jewish, Muslim or Hindu children; "those being nurtured in a Christian home."[36] Collins quotes C. S. Lewis to the effect that, since we cannot read other people's hearts to determine whether or not they are Christians, we

> must therefore stick to the original meaning. The name Christians was first given at Antioch (Acts xi. 26) to "the disciples," to those who accepted the teaching of the apostles. . . . When a man who accepts the Christian doctrine lives unworthily of it, it is much clearer to say he is a bad Christian than to say he is not a Christian.[37]

This obviously applies to adult believers, but the implications for their children are not hard to see.

---

34. Douma, *Infant Baptism and Regeneration*, 35 (italics original).

35. *Westminster Confession of Faith*, 382–84.

36. Wright, *Baptism*, 169.

37. Lewis, as quoted in Collins, "What Does Baptism Do?," 33.

INFANT BAPTISM/BABY DEDICATION

Based on historical research, David Wright suggests that early church practice allowed for various forms of infant dedication, as well as infant baptism.[38] In what proved to be Wright's last literary work, published posthumously and already quoted, *Baptism: Three Views*, Tony Lane also takes this position, as well as agreeing with Wright that the historical and biblical evidence supports a dual-practice approach to baptism. The other two contributors to this volume, Bruce Ware and Sinclair Ferguson, are dismissive of Lane's approach, considering it incoherent and naïve, as well as historically and biblically questionable. The arguments for and against can be read in the responses and counterresponses to Lane's essay, but given the New Testament emphasis on church unity (John 17:21; Eph 4:4), I find it difficult to argue with his conclusion:

> The New Testament practice of baptism was converts' baptism, the immediate baptism of those who come to faith as part of their initial response to the gospel. This needs to be modified for children born into a Christian home, either into infant baptism or into baptism at a later date. The New Testament evidence for how such children were treated is not unambiguous. Both approaches can be defended on biblical grounds. No grounds exist for insisting on one way to the exclusion of the other. The policy of accepting diversity is the only policy for which the first four centuries of the church provide any clear evidence.[39]

Lane notes further that in the contemporary situation:

> Many churches observe some sort of dedication ceremony after the birth of the child. This is followed by a

---

38. Wright, *Infant Baptism*, 116–38.

39. Wright, *Baptism*, 171. Leithart, in Strawbridge, *Case for Covenantal Infant Baptism*, offers an alternative (rather speculative) interpretation of the evidence, according to which covenantal infant baptism was apostolic practice and teaching, the first generation of biblically literate Jewish believers were all but wiped out in the destruction of Jerusalem in AD 70, and succeeding generations of baptismal rituals were influenced by Greek mystery religions (246–62).

period of Christian nurture. . . . If all goes well, it concludes with the grown-up child making a personal public profession of faith in baptism. In other churches the newborn baby is baptized. This is followed by a period of Christian nurture. . . . If all goes well, it concludes with a personal public profession of faith. . . which may or may not be called confirmation. . . . It is reasonable to regard both of the strategies outlined above as different, but legitimate, adaptations of the converts' baptism of Acts to the changed situation of the nurture of children in a Christian home. Both demand a program of Christian nurture which, in the last resort, is more important than any of the ceremonies.[40]

Lane acknowledges that many will regard this proposal as "hopelessly idealistic," but insists that this is not so:

In the first place, throughout the early church whenever we have clear evidence, the children of Christian families were baptized at every conceivable age.[41] . . . Second, many, if not most, paedobaptist churches today accept that not all Christian parents wish to have their children baptized. The churches make provision for alternative ceremonies such as dedication or blessing. . . . It is harder for Baptists to come to terms with this as many of them still regard infant baptism as no baptism at all, or at best highly irregular. . . . Finally, the dual practice approach has not been unknown in recent centuries.[42]

Here Lane references examples from the seventeenth century, as well as the present, that were mentioned earlier in chapter 2 of our study. The seventeenth-century example is of a "group of Baptist churches," which suggests that while it may be harder for Baptists than paedobaptists to accept a dual-practice approach, it is not impossible. I would add that it would only be possible with an understanding of infant baptism closer to "baby dedication with water" than to any of the alternatives.

---

40. Wright, *Baptism*, 163.

41. Lane provides the evidence for this in Wright, *Baptism*, 139–71.

42. Wright, *Baptism*, 164–65.

According to David Wright, building on the research of Hughes Oliphant Old and others, Martin Bucer (1491–1551) the Reformer of Strasbourg and later England, was a key figure in the development of evangelical confirmation as a "quasi-sacramental" completion of infant baptism.[43] Wright quotes Gottfried Hammann to the effect that for Bucer, "Baptism did not install the baptized—infant or adult—in a state, but integrated him into a dynamic body, enrolling him as a candidate in a process of Christian formation and spiritual development." This, Wright says, "also informed the development of the Strasbourg baptismal liturgy of 1537, with a direct address to the godparents to assist the parents in the nurture of the child and thus prove themselves 'spiritual fathers and mothers to him.'"[44]

In Roman Catholicism, confirmation is one of seven sacraments, but it remains quasi-sacramental in Protestant traditions that practice it. This becomes a problem when it happens as a matter of course at a given age, usually around thirteen or so, comparable to a Jewish *bar mitzvah* or *bat mitzvah*. The same applies to professions of faith in Reformed churches, which traditionally have taken place later, around the age of eighteen. Confirmation and dedication both have biblically questionable support. Both are substitutes for baptism, but confirmation has the added advantage of securing the right to partake of the Lord's Supper as the sacrament of nurture. A specific rite of confirmation cannot be proven to be biblically necessary, but may be justified as a step towards the goal of participating in the second sacrament.[45] In my own background, an interview with the elders was sufficient without a public profession of faith (other than that involved in actually partaking of the Lord's Supper). This seems eminently biblical.

Most Reformed Baptists, as well as paedobaptists, reject baby dedication as a poor substitute for infant baptism without clear

---

43. Wright, *Infant Baptism,* 371.

44. Wright, *Infant Baptism,* 176. Cf. Hammann, *Entre la secte,* 57.

45. Anecdotally, Gordon Fee has said that the baptism of infants or children is like an accordion. It may have started with a formal infant baptism event but the process was not complete until the individual made a confession of faith as an adult.

biblical warrant. The modern practice is thought to have developed in conjunction with the Sunday School movement coupled with "the natural Christian instinct of parents who did not agree with the biblical doctrine of infant baptism but desired to have a corresponding rite for their children."[46] Biblical support, it is suggested, can be found in the examples of Hannah bringing Samuel to the temple (1 Sam 1:24), Mary and Joseph in bringing the infant Jesus to the temple (Luke 2:22) and the mothers bringing their children to Jesus to be blessed (Luke 18:15 uses the word "babies").[47]

Paedobaptists point out that dedication focuses on the faith of the parents at the expense of the grace and promises of God in baptism. A common argument is that there is no better picture of the unmerited grace of God than a helpless infant, incapable of doing anything to merit divine favor. Thus, Henry DeMoor who taught Church Order at the CRC's Calvin Theological Seminary for many years, states in his *Church Order Commentary,* "nothing speaks of God's grace quite as profoundly as the water of baptism administered to an uncomprehending child."[48] This would be a powerful and convincing argument, except that it is nowhere used in the New Testament in connection with the practice of baptism, although it can perhaps be inferred from its theology. Barth notes that "the Reformers made no use of this argument, and we may say that it

---

46. Najapfour, *Child Dedication*, 33.

47. Najapfour, himself a former Baptist, exegetes these passages referenced and finds that they do not provide adequate biblical support for child dedication. However, while not mandated in Scripture, dedication "can serve to bind the dedicators to honoring the Lord" (30). Najapfour hopes to "encourage those who practice baby dedication to consider the Reformed doctrine of infant baptism" (34).

48. DeMoor, *Christian Reformed Church Order Commentary*, 308. See also Douma, who writes, "Do we not point out to the Reformed Baptists what for them, too, is the heart of the gospel when we criticize their rejection of infant baptism?" (*Infant Baptism and Regeneration*, 36.) John Stott notes that Articles 25, 27, and 28 of the 39 Articles of the Church of England "all begin with the statement that a sacrament is a sign not of what we do or are, but of what God has done or does" (Stott and Motyer, *Anglican Evangelical Doctrine of Infant Baptism*, 7.) See also, "the sheer gratuitousness of the grace of salvation is particularly manifest in infant baptism," (*Catechism of the Catholic Church,* Part Two, Section Two, Chapter One, Article 1, para 1250.)

could be convincing only if the justification for infant baptism was already proved."[49] Lane says, "This theme owes much to Reformed theology, little to the New Testament."[50] The stress on New Testament missionary baptism is on the faith of the convert responding to God's offer of salvation. Besides, the faith of the baptized believer is no less a sovereign gift of grace, such that the response of faith implies the prior existence of regenerating grace. As D. L. Migliore points out, referring to an objective reality view (emphasizing grace) and a subjective reality view (emphasizing faith), the first view is in danger of minimizing "the importance of the response of faith. . . . The danger of the subjective view is that it obscures the unconditional and objective reality of God's grace."[51]

To be sure, infant baptism involves not *first* our dedicating our children to God, but claiming his covenant promises as the one initiating the relationship so established. Perhaps the idea of infant blessing rather than dedication captures more the thought of the divine initiative.[52] However, there is a fair amount of support for seeing dedication as "the second half" of baptism.[53] For instance, the baptismal vows of the Presbyterian Church in America (PCA),

---

49. Barth, *Learning Jesus through the Heidelberg Catechism*, 104.

50. Wright, *Baptism*, 126.

51. Migliore, *Faith Seeking Understanding*, 212–13.

52. In a provocatively titled article, "The True Calvinist," van der Leer ends with a quote from the Reformed theologian Sake Stoppels, "in which he pleads for exchanging infant baptism for infant blessing, and 'to reserve baptism for the moment that believers decide to devote themselves to God, His Kingdom and the fellowship of the people who also want to do so'" (28). Cf. Stoppels, "Een kerk met gastvrije drempels," 236.

53. This terminology is taken from the Rev. Ken Koeman's (1942–2018) answer to a letter in the Q & A page of *The Banner* (the denominational magazine of the CRC) in August 18, 1997: "Dedication is the second half of baptism. Baptism is God speaking to the child, promising him or her the blessings of the covenant, promises claimed and treasured by the parents. Dedication is the response of the parents, placing the child into the hands of God and promising to train him or her in the gospel. . . . But without baptism, dedication loses the solid foundation of God's promises that gives it substance and purpose. It's like a wedding in which only the bride gives the ring." DeMoor also speaks of dedication as the "lesser half" of baptism (*Christian Reformed Church Order Commentary*, 310).

influenced more by J. H. Thornwell's Sothern Presbyterian view
than by Hodge's in the north (see more later in chapter 5), ask three
questions, the last of which is:

> Do you now unreservedly dedicate your child to God,
> and promise, in humble reliance upon divine grace, that
> you will endeavor to set before (him) a godly example,
> that you will pray with and for (him), that you will teach
> (him) the doctrines of our holy religion, and that you will
> strive, by all the means of God's appointment, to bring
> (him) up in the nurture and admonition of the Lord?[54]

Likewise, Archibald Alexander of Princeton (1772–1851)
spoke of parents "about to dedicate [their children] to God in holy
baptism" praying earnestly "that they might be baptized with the
Holy Ghost."[55] Alexander goes on to speak of this as a form of
baptismal regeneration, language Cunningham would have clearly
rejected, but the point is that Alexander understood baptism as at
least in part a form of dedication. Similarly, Charles Hodge, who
was referenced earlier as teaching presumptive election, could also
state that ". . . all such professors of the true religion are bound to
present their children for baptism as the divinely appointed way of
consecrating them to God."[56]

To quote another authority from the past, with present-day
relevance, Richard Baxter (1615–91) whose overall defense of infant baptism J. I. Packer describes as speaking for the Puritan movement in general,[57] states:

> I have oft shewed *that If our Childrens* (sic) *part in the
> Covenant of Grace upon their Parents dedication of them
> to God and so their Church-membership,* were but yielded,
> the rest (whether they should actually be *Baptized with
> Water*) would be much less cause of our distance and

---

54. *The Book of Church Order (PCA)*, ch. 56, para. 5. The gender-specific
language is in the original.

55. Alexander, *Thoughts on Religious Experience*, 12–13.

56. Hodge, *Systematic Theology*, 3:562. I am indebted to William Barker for
drawing my attention to this statement.

57. "Indeed, in the Baptist controversy, his fellow-Puritans regarded him as
a champion of their cause" (Packer, *Redemption and Restoration of Man*, 285).

alienation, than on both sides it is usually judged. Yea, if the Anabaptists would but say, [*I Dedicate this Child to God, as far as he hath given me power, and heartily desire that God may be his Father, Christ his Saviour, and the Holy Spirit his Sanctifier*]: And did ever any of you prove this to be a sin? And we are ready on our part to profess that [*Infant-Baptism will save none at age, that confess not to the same holy Covenant*].[58]

Packer says of Baxter's position,

As in other legal agreements, so in God's covenant, parents are entitled to pledge their children as well as themselves. The child's right to baptism has thus a double foundation: his parentage, the fact that he is a child of professing Christians which makes him eligible for it, and his parents' actual decision to dedicate him to God, which makes it his due.[59]

Baxter repeatedly stressed the need for faith as a condition for baptism.[60] So much was this the case that one of the few cases in which he would consider rebaptism to be valid was if parental faith were lacking the first time.[61] Contemporaries such as John Tombes (1603?–76) and Henry Danvers (d. 1687) among others, argued that to be consistent, Baxter's convictions on the necessity of faith should logically lead him to abandon his belief in infant baptism. Baxter, however, saw no inconsistency in his position. He held that in infant baptism the believing parent acts in "his infant's part."[62] A similar emphasis of a more recent nature on the role of parental faith can be found in *What about Baptism?* by the late Robert Rayburn (1915–90), founding president of Covenant Theological Seminary, in which position he served from 1956–77.[63]

---

58. Baxter, *Rich. Baxter's review*, (sic), 4 (italics and brackets in the original).

59. Packer, *Redemption and Restoration of Man*, 280.

60. Baxter, *Practical Works of Richard Baxter*, 1:651.

61. Baxter, *Practical Works of Richard Baxter*, 1:662.

62. Baxter, *Practical Works of Richard Baxter*, 1:651.

63. Rayburn, *What about Baptism?*, chs. 8 and 9.

Hans Boersma comments that Baxter's insistence that "parents . . . are able to profess saving faith on behalf of their children" illustrates "the unique position of Baxter among paedobaptists in maintaining that the basis of baptism does not lie exclusively in the promise of God, nor in the (presumed) regeneration of the child, but in the justifying faith of the parents."[64] This alleged uniqueness of Baxter's position conflicts with Packer's evaluation that Baxter's "fellow-Puritans regarded him as a champion of their cause."[65] It also conflicts with the later view of Cunningham and others as discussed previously in chapter 3.

Packer adopted a position much like that of Lane above:

> The Christian nurture of baptist and paedobaptist children will be similar:dedicated to God in infancy, either by baptism or by a dedication rite (which some will see as a dry baptism), they will then be brought up to live for the Lord and led to publicly professing faith on their own account in confirmation or baptism (which some will see as a wet confirmation).[66]

Sinclair Ferguson, in response to Lane's dual-practice position, states that "Some of the arguments used by credobaptists against the baptism of infants tell also against the dedication of their own children." For instance, "The child must make its own decision about Christ. How then can the parents make it in infant dedication?" Ferguson then continues that, in effect, "the service of infant dedication turns out either to share paedobaptist theology, but not see it through to an appropriate conclusion . . . or to be a dedication of the parents, but not of the infant."[67] Reformed Baptists, who with Reformed paedobaptists stress the priority of divine grace in salvation, often reject infant dedication on such grounds. This is why it might be better to speak of the blessing of children (which Jesus clearly did). However, if we take the approach to dedication in the third question of the PCA's baptismal vows (see above), there

---

64. Boersma, *Richard Baxter's Understanding of Infant Baptism*, 54.

65. Packer, *Redemption and Restoration of Man*, 285.

66. Packer, *Concise Theology*, 215–16.

67. Wright, *Baptism*, 184.

is nothing there to which believing Baptist parents of whichever variety would not wish to commit in principle. If not evidence of an implicitly shared paedobaptist theology, perhaps we could speak of a similar theology of children with those who practice dedication.

There are in fact denominations that, at least in theory, allow for dual practice of infant baptism and baby dedication. Ken Stewart and Tony Lane, as noted previously, mention a few in the past as well as present.[68] David Wright references the United Reformed Church in England and Scotland the Church of North India, as well as some independent churches in England, and the French Reformed Church, and notes that this policy "has even to a limited sense been at least condoned by one or two bishops in the Church of England."[69] Some of these references take us beyond what are normally considered to be evangelical and Reformed churches (the United Reformed Church, for instance, is generally more liberal than historically Reformed, and the same can be said of the Church of England.) However, within evangelicalism, I was interested to learn that a minority of Pentecostal groups practice both believers' and infant baptism and this "may prove to be particularly useful in interchurch discussions."[70] In particular, Simon G. H. Tan argues that believers' baptism is a practice uniquely suited to western individualism and does not resonate in Asian cultures that are closer to those of biblical times. Tan goes so far as to reject the biblical warrant for the more common practice (in Pentecostal circles) of baby dedication as an alternative to infant baptism, although he seems to indicate (like Packer) that it is "a kind of baptism without water!"[71]

---

68. Stewart, *In Search of Ancient Roots*, 136. See also Finn above, ch. 2n7.

69. Wright, *Infant Baptism*, 277–78.

70. Robeck Jr. and Sandidge, as quoted in Williams, "Water Baptism in Pentecostal Perspective," 72.

71. Tan, "Reassessing Believer's Baptism," 232 (italics original). Lane likewise points out that "for the modern Westerner we are all individuals who must make our own decisions for ourselves. . . . This is self-evident to us. It is not so self-evident to other cultures, and it is anachronistic to suppose that the first-century Christians thought that way. It is not a coincidence that the *principled rejection* of infant baptism, the belief that it is wrong, originated in the sixteenth century, at a time when individualism was becoming stronger in the West" (Wright, *Baptism*, 63). At the same time, while paedobaptists "bear

Dedication, it should be said, is often associated with a so-called "age of innocence" prior to an "age of accountability," the idea being that children who die before they reach an age of accountability are not held responsible for their sins and so go to heaven. There is no universally recognized age of accountability, but it is sometimes put at the age of thirteen based on the Jewish practice of coming of age (*bar mitzvah* for males, *bat mitzvah* for females). The Bible does not directly teach an age of accountability, but some rather curious exegesis is used to support it, such as reading into Paul's statement in Romans 7:9 about once being "alive apart from the law" that this was a reference to his age of innocence. Another supposed support is Isaiah 7:16 and its reference to a time before the promised Immanuel knows enough "to reject the wrong and choose the right," obviously in context, an allusion to the prophet's son rather than the ultimate fulfillment in the coming of Christ. It should not be difficult to see how forced these interpretations are, and when Reformed Baptists reject baby dedication on these grounds, they are right to do so. However, the practice of dedication need not be tied to these questionable ideas.

Interestingly, there appears to be a move in the direction of permitting dedication as an alternative to baptism among some in the present Free Church of Scotland. It might be argued that this is a logical development of Cunningham's view, although I suspect he would have preferred a universally understood explanation of infant baptism as incorporating a form of dedication. Donald Macleod has expressed strong opposition to "a growing demand for Baptist style Services of Dedication for Infants" in the Free Church.[72] Macleod, in my view, is ably refuted by David Robertson in "The Downgrade of the Free Church—A response to Donald Macleod."[73] Macleod expresses a common view elsewhere when, after acknowledging

---

witness against the individualism of the postmodern age and point to God's dealing with families. . . . Baptists by contrast bear witness against the scourge of nominal Christianity and remind us that in the strict sense God has no grandchildren" (167).

72. Macleod, "Should Presbyterians Have Dedication Services?," para. 1.

73. Robertson, "Downgrade of the Free Church." See also Robertson, "When the Levy Breaks."

that the debate between Baptists and paedobaptists is not about fundamentals, he continues, "There is no doubt that it is difficult to have the two points of view co-existing in one church or denomination, but that is a practical, not a theological, difficulty."[74] I agree with him when he also states that "the children of our Baptist friends are as much covenant-children as our own. The fact of their not being baptised does not mean they are not covenant-children. It means only that the sign of the covenant is not put upon them."[75] But when Macleod references Presbyterians and Anglicans preaching in Baptist churches as evidence of theological compatibility, is this enough? Baptists and paedobaptists also work happily together in parachurch organizations, agreeing to differ on the issue of baptism, as well as other matters. But parachurch organizations, with their limited statements of faith, are a testimony to the failure of the organized church to achieve the structural unity and witness that Jesus prayed for in John 17:21.

I would suggest that it is only on Cunningham's understanding of infant baptism, rather than any other (such as presumptive election or regeneration), that progress can be made in recognizing the unity among evangelical Christians (who are my primary target audience) of the church's "one Lord, one faith, one baptism" (Eph 4:5).

74. Macleod, *Faith to Live By*, 229.
75. Macleod, *Faith to Live By*, 235.

5

Missionary Baptism and
Covenant Children

AT THE END OF chapter 3, the question was raised: If household missionary baptism was a New Testament practice, "What then of children growing up in Christian families, which is the norm in both Baptist and paedobaptist churches today?" We have seen that Cunningham believed they should be presumed nonregenerate (the reverse of presumptive regeneration) before conversion. Is this the safest policy, or does it not take seriously enough their privileged status as "covenant children"? Would it be better to say with Douma, "You are a Christian child. . . . Repent and believe the gospel"?[1] Sinclair Ferguson pointed out that although children from Christian families may not experience conversion as a moment of psychological crisis, "The gospel sign of baptism—whether received in infancy or in later years on profession of faith—calls all to . . . lifelong conversion."[2] To introduce a similar perspective, in a booklet called *How Our Children Come to Faith*, Stephen Smallman suggests that *discipleship* of children better fits the admonition of Ephesians 6:4 than *evangelism* in terms of leading covenant children to Christ. He writes:

---

1. See Douma, *Infant Baptism and Regeneration*, 35.
2. Wright, *Baptism*, 111.

Do our children need to be converted? The answer to that is yes, as long as we don't define conversion as some kind of experience. . . . The earliest disciples were following Jesus even while they were learning what it means to believe in him. Can't it be said that our children are part of a family of Jesus' disciples and that in that sense, they themselves are also disciples?[3]

JOEL R. BEEKE

I find it helpful to turn back to Joel Beeke, whom I quoted in chapter 1 from his short book, *Bringing the Gospel to Covenant Children*. He subsequently wrote a much longer volume, *Parenting By God's Promises*. Among other things, he discusses the status of believers' children. Not surprisingly, given his background and opposition to presumptive regeneration, he begins by asserting that they are *sinners*. This, of course, is not disputed by Christians of all stripes, but in Beeke's background (and in the one in which I grew up) it tends to be the defining characteristic at the expense of any others. Beeke, however, proceeds to provide a more balanced approach. He states that as God's representatives, seeking to reflect his character and the fruit of his Spirit in our relationship with our children,

we also remember that our children are not our own; they belong to Him. . . . He has a claim on them as covenant children, even in their unregenerate state, just as He had a claim on all the children of Israel. It was for this reason that God rebuked . . . the sin of Jewish parents sacrificing their children to idols, saying, "Thou hast slain my children" (Ezek. 16:21).[4]

To this might be added Malachi 2:15, with its emphasis on spiritual unity in marriage producing godly offspring (seed in KJV).

Beeke quotes the Dutch Reformed Form for the Administration of Baptism which says, "We with our children are conceived and born in sin, and therefore are children of wrath, inasmuch as

3. Smallman, *How Our Children Come to Faith*, 20–22.
4. Beeke, *Parenting by God's Promises*, 16.

we cannot enter the kingdom of God except we are born again."[5] The same form goes on to ask the parents "First, Whether you acknowledge, that although our children are conceived and born in sin, and therefore are subject to all miseries, yea, to condemnation itself; yet that they are sanctified in Christ, and therefore, as members of his Church ought to be baptized?"[6] This follows the traditional Reformed understanding of 1 Corinthians 7:14, "For the unbelieving husband is sanctified by the wife, and the unbelieving wife is sanctified by the husband; else were your children unclean; but now they are holy" (KJV). What does this mean for the children of marriages where at least one parent is a professing believer? In what does the holiness of such children consist? Beeke answers this in the by-now-familiar language of God's covenant promises to believers and their children. He discusses three views.[7] The first is that the holiness of children is *internal and saving*. This means that they are presumed to be regenerate at birth or soon after. I quoted his opposition to this view in chapter 1, but I think it bears repeating in the way he puts it here:

> The fruits of this view can be quite tragic. Children are not taught that they must be born again. Instead they are treated as part of the family of God from the beginning. As a result, many grow up as nominal members of the church, thinking they are saved. They believe Reformed church doctrines and perform their duties as church members, but often appear to be strangers to the experiential inner life of grace. Knowing God personally is replaced with "kingdom activities" of family, church,

---

5. Beeke, *Parenting by God's Promises*, 17.

6. *Reformed Liturgy*. The wording is slightly updated in one of the forms used in the CRC, but the substance is the same in all branches of Dutch Reformed Christianity, although with different interpretations.

7. There are actually more than three views of 1 Cor 7:14 and not all of them relate the holiness of children to their baptismal status. Melanchthon, for instance, understood this passage as meaning that the children born to a mixed marriage are not illegitimate. Wright references "a recent summary" that "lists six possible solutions, and regards as most persuasive the view that sanctification is what makes the marriage relationship pure, thus removing grounds for dissolution" (Wright, *Infant Baptism*, 209).

school, and community life. So much stress is laid on the privilege of inclusion in the covenant that it obviates the need for regeneration, true conversion, or any other part of personal Christian experience.[8]

It is not entirely clear to me how being treated as part of the family of God from the beginning differs from saying that believers' children belong to God and he lays claim to them (which Beeke affirms). It also bears repeating that the "tragic" outcomes Beeke notes are not universally the case. Besides, in the Dutch Reformed tradition he represents (as well as in Scottish Highland piety), there can be an overemphasis on the need for conversion experiences that becomes paralyzing for those who have not had such an experience and so conclude that they are not saved even though they give every evidence of true faith. This can lead to an obsession with seeking assurance of salvation at the expense of active Christian service. Nevertheless, the dangers Beeke warns of are real and can indeed be tragic. Abraham Kuyper's colleague, Herman Bavinck, agreed that in the judgment of charity, baptized children should be regarded as "elect and regenerate unless their conduct and life give evidence to the contrary,"[9] but he resisted the idea that this was the *ground* of baptism and it is his qualifications that are reflected in the language of the "Conclusions of Utrecht."[10] He also understood and shared the concern that "It seems as though even when a person has continued living for years in an unconverted state, he still must be considered to be regenerated."[11]

The second view Beeke discusses he characterizes as the Baptist position. It is *external, not covenantal.* This means that children of believers have only "an external sanctity or legitimacy as the offspring and heirs of their parents." Of this view, Beeke comments:

> One might think that this view would tend to lead parents to regard their children as heathen, cut off from God

---

8. Beeke, *Parenting by God's Promises*, 19.

9. Beach, "Abraham Kuyper, Herman Bavinck," 51. Cf. Bavinck, *Reformed Dogmatics*, 4:57n36; 68, 80, 530–32.

10. See p. 4 above.

11. Bavinck, *Saved by Grace*, 4.

and excluded from His church. The good news is that many Baptists, despite their weak view of the covenant, raise their children as if they were covenant children. In fact they sometimes do a better job than those in Reformed churches. . . . I admire the way many Reformed Baptists rear their children, even though I disagree with them at this point in their theology.[12]

Beeke devotes a chapter to infant baptism and, despite his avowed admiration for the way many Reformed Baptists rear their children, gives no indication that the Reformed Baptist view of the covenant of grace, particularly of the circumcision/baptism analogy, is any different from other Baptist views. This is disappointing but does not detract from the fact that many Baptists, Reformed or otherwise, intentionally raise their children for Christ despite their rejection of infant baptism (or dedication, for that matter).

The third and final view "is held by many Reformed and Presbyterian churches." It is *external and covenantal,* meaning that children of believers "have a physical and external relationship to the covenant from birth. God has extended His promises to them as well as to their parents, but these promises must be embraced with believing hearts. Covenant children cannot experience the truth and power of these promises so long as they are unregenerate, unbelieving, and impenitent." This view "maintains a balance between the first two views, thereby neither overestimating nor underestimating the covenant."[13]

God's normal way of adding to his church is "by saving the children of believers. He does not promise to save all children raised by Christians, but it is His ordinary way to save them over a period of time. He has promised to raise up a seed to serve him from generation to generation." God does

also save people from unchurched and noncovenantal families, but this is not as usual as conversion within church families. When it does happen, the converted person enters the covenant by joining the church as a

---

12. Beeke, *Parenting by God's Promises*, 20.

13. Beeke, *Parenting by God's Promises*, 21.

confessing member, then potentially marrying within the church and raising a family in the church, so that the process of raising covenantal children goes on.[14]

Thus, Beeke encourages an attitude of cautious optimism in the raising of covenant children. He wisely notes that, while we should reject presumptive regeneration, we should not go to the opposite extreme and embrace presumptive *non*regeneration. While it is possible "to do more harm than good if we treat children who make tentative professions of faith as if they were truly saved" without waiting for "evidence of their transformation before flooding them with assurances," on the other hand, "we can be too skeptical. If a child is truly saved and we refuse to acknowledge his or her new standing before God, we can seriously discourage a new believer. Also, we must not expect such children suddenly to act like adults, for their spiritual experiences are usually commensurate with their age."[15]

There is much wisdom here, fleshed out in practical ways in the rest of the book. Since church planting is often the most effective means of church growth, it might be questioned whether God's normal method of adding to the church is by the salvation of believers' children who are already in the church. But if Beeke's assertion to that effect is true, it applies to the baptism of children in Baptist churches as much as to the profession of faith of those in Reformed churches. Should this be the case though? As Ken Stewart pointed out, "Does not the very frequency with which infant baptism is practiced in our churches practically obscure our failure to evangelize and baptize from the world?"[16] One of the New Testament images of the church is the family of God, but too often it becomes a collection of families, comfortable and familiar with one another, who become ingrown to the point that outsiders feel unwelcome. The New Testament pattern was of families entering the church by baptism. This continues in pioneering missionary situations and also in periods of spiritual revival when unbelievers

---

14. Beeke, *Parenting by God's Promises*, 23–24.

15. Beeke, *Parenting by God's Promises*, 27.

16. See Stewart, *In Search of Ancient Roots*, 139.

and nominal church members alike have come under the power of the gospel and are converted. Perhaps we have too little expectation of this happening in connection with our evangelistic endeavors, but ultimately it is the sovereign work of God's Spirit to add to the church "such as should be saved" (Acts 2:47 KJV).

Meanwhile, whether by conversion or Christian nurture from generation to generation, it remains that God extends his grace to the children of believers who are brought up "in the training and instruction of the Lord" (Eph 6:4b ESV). As Donald Macleod acknowledges for all his opposition to baby dedication, this is true of "covenant children" whether or not baptized in infancy.[17]

The Heritage Reformed Congregations, of which Beeke is the most recognized leader, are unique among Reformed churches of Dutch origin in that they subscribe not only to the Three Forms of Unity (the Heidelberg Catechism, the Belgic Confession and the Canons of Dordt) but also to the Westminster Confession and Catechisms, on which William Cunningham mostly built his argument, as discussed previously. The Heidelberg Catechism, which corresponds most closely to the Shorter Catechism, devotes several questions and answers to the subject of baptism. Q & A 69–73, much like the Shorter Catechism, appear to be discussing the meaning of baptism for believers, stressing that water baptism represents the cleansing of the blood of Christ by the Holy Spirit. Then there is an abrupt shift to the covenant basis of infant baptism. Infants, as much as adults, are promised "deliverance from sin through Christ's blood and the Holy Spirit who produces faith." There is no mention of the parents' role or of any conditionality to the promises made. This can (although clearly not in Beeke's case) lead to an understanding of infant baptism in terms of something like presumptive regeneration and a consequent rejection of their baptism by some, as well as a nominal faith by others.[18] Granted,

---

17. Some would object to this by pointing to the Lord's attempt to kill Moses in Exod 4:24–26, apparently for having failed to circumcise his sons, and drawing a parallel with the seriousness of infant baptism, but it should be apparent by now that I judge this not to be an exact parallel.

18. Zacharias Ursinus, thought to be the principal author of the Heidelberg Catechism, writes that baptized infants of believers have an "inclination

as the Heidelberg Catechism also states, the children of believers should be "distinguished from the children of unbelievers," perhaps even called Christian children (as in the Westminster Directory for the Publick Worship of God). However, it would have been clearer if the catechism had made the point that baptism is for *believers and their children*. (To its credit, one of the CRC baptismal forms does make this point, even if it is not the major emphasis.)

The late Fred Klooster (1922–2003), in his magisterial two-volume commentary on the Heidelberg Catechism, notes that the catechism's "discussion of baptism could well have been enriched by references to faith." He also recognizes that Q&A 69 (defining baptism as an outward washing of water representing the washing away of sin by the blood and Spirit of Christ) "is directed to one who is already a believer in Christ." Further, "there is no indication whether this question applies to children as well as adults." In fact, some favor the view that Q&A 69–73 "have only adult baptism in mind." Even if this is so, "it is still a fact that answer 74 has retroactive significance, and it is wise to bear this in mind when discussing Q&A's 69–74." In other words, the baptized infants of believers, by virtue of their participation in the covenant of grace, in the language of answer 74, are "no less than adults . . . promised the forgiveness of sin through Christ's blood and the Holy Spirit who produces faith."[19]

One difference between the Westminster Catechisms and the Heidelberg is that the questions of the Heidelberg are addressed in the second person singular and answered in the first person,

---

to faith" and "If infants now have the Holy Ghost, he certainly works in them regeneration, good inclinations, new desires, and such other things as are necessary for their salvation, or he at least supplies them with every thing (*sic*) that is requisite for their baptism" (*Commentary of Zacharias Ursinus on the Heidelberg Catechism,* 370).

Bierma, in discussing the views of Caspar Olevianus, thought to be a co-author with Ursinus, notes: "It is the Holy Spirit who purifies, not the water. But he will go so far as to say that the water of baptism is more than mere water (*schlect wasser*), for the water is so bound to the promise of God that the physical cleansing becomes if not the instrument at least the occasion for the spiritual cleansing" (*German Calvinism in the Confessional Age,* 87).

19. Klooster, *Our Only Comfort,* 2:794, 790, 807.

meaning that the person answering is not simply reciting objective doctrine, but subjectively claiming the promises of baptism as well as of other doctrines. This presents a difficulty for those who are not prepared to admit that the children of believers are presumed to be believers themselves by the time they are able to recite the answers, since, like other post-Reformation catechisms, the Heidelberg was originally intended to teach children as well as to provide a basis for catechism preaching. Various solutions have been found. Herman Hoeksema (1886–1965), co-founder of the Protestant Reformed Churches in 1924, taught that the catechism is addressed to the "spiritual seed" (i.e., the elect) among those who have been baptized. The "carnal seed is not addressed, it is left out of view."[20] The obvious difficulty with this is that it is impossible for mere mortals to determine infallibly who is or is not elect. Beeke's approach is to understand the catechism, as well as other confessions and baptismal forms, as presenting the ideal situation. He also believes that, by God's sovereign, covenantal grace, the conversion of covenant children should be the norm—that it is "normative for those who have been brought up faithfully by believing parents in a diligent use of the means of grace, for the Holy Spirit to bless those means to their conversion at some point in their childhood, teen, or young adult years."[21]

LEWIS BEVENS SCHENCK

It is interesting to compare Beeke's view with that of Lewis Bevens Schenck (1898–1985) in his classic *The Presbyterian Doctrine of Children in the Covenant*. Schenck believed presumptive regeneration to be the traditional Reformed and Presbyterian view from Calvin on, including the Westminster Confession of Faith.[22]

---

20. Hoeksema, *Triple Knowledge*, 1:25. Hoeksema's view of "covenant baptism" is explained in his *Believers and Their Seed*. He held that only the elect were included in the covenant of grace. The normative rule was for covenant children to be regenerated in early childhood, but come to faith later in life.

21. Based on personal conversation on Zoom, December 15, 2020, and an email of January 31, 2021.

22. Schenck, *Presbyterian Doctrine*, ch. 1. Others have claimed that Calvin

In his view, the Great Awakening in the eighteenth century was responsible for a change in emphasis such that covenant children were now regarded as unregenerate and in need of conversion, just as much as the children of unbelievers.[23] "It was unfortunate that the Great Awakening made an emotional experience, involving terror, misery, and depression, the only approach to God. A conscious conversion from enmity to friendship with God was looked upon as the only way of entrance into the kingdom."[24] These elements applied even to the conversion of young children:

> The childish fright and pitiful terror of children of God like these and the element of fear in their conception of God aroused the sympathy of some and incited the indignation of a few. But if the objection was raised to the unscriptural and detrimental emotional strain of such a "convicting and converting" experience for children, the reply was simply that it was necessary.[25]

The effects of the Great Awakening carried over into the nineteenth century, leading to a devaluation of infant baptism. A view of the Abrahamic covenant developed such that the children of believers were in a visible ecclesiastical covenant with Abraham, but were not yet partakers of the spiritual internal covenant of grace. "Thus

---

taught a form of baptismal regeneration. For a helpful refutation of this, as well as that Calvin taught presumptive regeneration, see Cassidy, "Calvin on Baptism," 534–54. Cassidy shows that Calvin made a distinction between the sign (*signa*) and the thing signified (*res*).

23. In a perceptive review of Schenck's book, Ken Stewart notes that he relied too much on the "objective" aspects of the teaching of the Reformers on infant baptism. "They have far more to say about the Holy Spirit's inward or effectual call in the subsequent life of the child than Schenck's interpretation suggests." The same is true of the Westminster Confession of Faith (WCF) which reflected seventeenth-century Puritan views in the century before the Great Awakening. (Stewart, "Review of Lewis B. Schenck," 124–26.) It might be added that the common charge of "preparationism" made against at least some Puritans (although not the WCF) is similar to the excesses Schenck attributes to the Great Awakening. Certainly, they were concerned about personal conversion. One need only read Baxter's *Call to the Unconverted* in conjunction with his defense of infant baptism to see how the two priorities relate to one another.

24. Schenck, *Presbyterian Doctrine*, 71.

25. Schenck, *Presbyterian Doctrine*, 66–67.

the visible church was not a group of those who were presumably true children of God, but a field out of which the true children of God were called, an institution in which they were trained. Naturally, it was supposed that this external relationship would serve as a means of transition to the internal covenant."[26]

Things came to a head in 1857, when the General Assembly of the Presbyterian Church in the United States of America gave the work of revising the Book of Discipline to a committee of eminent theologians, among them Charles Hodge of Princeton Seminary and James Henley Thornwell (1812–62) of Columbia Seminary. Thornwell prepared a draft which proposed changing the language that all baptized members are "members of the church" and "subject to its government and discipline." The revised wording stated that all baptized persons were under the church's "government and training," but "only those, however, who have made a profession of faith in Christ are proper subjects of judicial prosecution."[27]

The proposed revision was presented to the General Assembly in 1859 and was strongly opposed by Hodge. His concern was not so much whether or not a baptized child was subject to the particular form of discipline implied in "judicial procedure," but that the child's "amenability to such process is denied on grounds which, as it seems to us, involve the denial of his true relation to the Church." He was, therefore, "decidedly in favour of the paragraph as it stands in our present Book."[28]

The debate dragged on and was interrupted by the Civil War. Following the resulting division into the Presbyterian Church USA (north) and the Presbyterian Church in the Confederate States of America (south), later renamed the Presbyterian Church US, the northern church restored the original wording of the Book of Discipline "with a slight addition in reference to the general sense of discipline."[29] The southern church, at its first General Assembly in 1861, appointed a committee, to be chaired by Thornwell, to

---

26. Schenck, *Presbyterian Doctrine*, 86.

27. Dabney, as quoted in Schenck, *Presbyterian Doctrine*, 90.

28. Hodge, as quoted in Schenck, *Presbyterian Doctrine*, 98.

29. Schenck, *Presbyterian Doctrine*, 100.

complete the proposed revision. Thornwell died before a meeting could be held. He was replaced in 1863 by John B. Adger (1810–99), and the revision was finally adopted in 1879.[30]

Schenck devotes a chapter to "The Defense of the Doctrine of Children in the Covenant." Here he relies heavily on Princeton theologians such as Hodge and B. B. Warfield (1851–1921), although Abraham Kuyper (*inter alia*) is also mentioned, writing in *The Presbyterian Quarterly*.[31] The doctrine of presumptive regeneration (or in Hodge's case, presumptive election) is reasserted with the qualification that "Although the time of their regeneration was not presumed, children of believers were thought by Princeton theologians and many others to be the true children of God."[32]

Christian nurture was deemed to be the "great means for the salvation of the children of the church."[33] Henry J. Van Dyke (1822–91), Pastor of First Presbyterian Church, Brooklyn, New York, in his 1890 Stone Lectures at Princeton, said, "Christian Nurture, beginning in infancy, inheriting traditional influences and surrounded at the first dawn of consciousness by a religious atmosphere, is the normal and divine method for propagating the Church."[34] Samuel Miller (1769–1850) of Princeton believed that:

---

30. Schenck, *Presbyterian Doctrine*, 101. The distinction between the northern and southern churches no longer applies geographically, but its influence can still be felt in the various divisions that have taken place since the nineteenth century and since Schenck's book was first published in 1940. For instance, the Orthodox Presbyterian Church (founded 1936), whose roots are in northern Presbyterianism, reflects that influence in its Book of Church Order and baptismal vows (which are very similar to those in the CRC), whereas the Presbyterian Church in America (founded 1973), with roots in the southern church, reflects more of Thornwell's influence in its officially approved baptismal vows, although individual churches and ministers may differ, some for historical reasons that would take us too far afield.

31. See Kuyper, "Calvinism and Confessional Revision," 503. Also, Warfield, "Polemics of Infant Baptism," 331.

32. Schenck, *Presbyterian Doctrine*, 140. The Princeton men overall took a more balanced approach to the Great Awakening than Schenck indicates, opposing its excesses but affirming the obvious spiritual and societal good that resulted.

33. Schenck, *Presbyterian Doctrine*, 142.

34. Van Dyke, as quoted in Schenck, *Presbyterian Doctrine*, 142.

The truth is, if infant baptism were properly improved, if the profession which it includes, and the obligations which it imposes, were suitably appreciated, and followed up, it would have few opponents. I can no more doubt, if this were done, that it would be blessed to the saving conversion of thousands of our young people, than I can doubt the faithfulness of a covenanted God. Yes, infant baptism is of God, but the fault lies in the conduct of its advocates. The inconsistencies of its friends has done more to discredit it, than all the arguments of its opposers, a hundred fold.[35]

Note the need for conversion mentioned here. In the normal course of events, according to Miller, Van Dyke, and others, this should take place as the result of the blessing of God on the Christian nurture of children rather than by a dramatic conversion experience. Whatever their other differences in their formulations of the covenant of grace in the case of children, this differs not at all with what Beeke advocated, and which he admits also takes place in the case of children raised in Baptist families. Miller's concern about the abuse of infant baptism also resonates with the concerns expressed by David Wright, although of course the Princeton theologians would not have agreed with Wright (or Cunningham) on the normativity of believers' baptism. All are agreed that while Christian nurture does not automatically guarantee saving grace, it is the usual method God uses with children of believing parents, and it is often its neglect that brings infant baptism into disrepute. In the case of children who come into the church in later childhood as a result of missionary baptism upon the conversion of one or both of their parents, the challenge may be greater, but the change of lifestyle involved (however it may be resisted at first) is a powerful testimony and example to the children.

---

35. Miller, as quoted in Schenck, *Presbyterian Doctrine*, 142–43.

THE CRC AND CHILD COMMUNION

Returning to the CRC, it has, like some other Reformed denominations, moved in the direction of permitting, but not requiring, the participation of covenant children at an early age in the celebration of the Lord's Supper. This is intended to be under the supervision of the elders and in some cases it is, but in others the decision is left entirely to the parents.[36] One reason for this development has been a growing conviction that Baptists were right in their criticism that paedobaptists are inconsistent in practicing infant baptism based on the covenant continuity between Israel and the church, but not allowing baptized children to take part in communion until they are old enough to make a personal profession of faith. The New Testament in a number of places indicates the need for faith and repentance prior to baptism, but paedobaptists reply that this applies to new converts and not to the infant children of believers. Likewise, 1 Corinthians 11 clearly teaches the need for self-examination before participating in the Lord's Supper, but advocates of paedocommunion are now saying this applies only to those old enough to do so. It does not refer to young children who have a right to participate by virtue of their membership in the covenant of grace. After all, it is argued, young children took part in the Passover, which originated as a family meal, so by analogy they should take part in the Lord's Supper, which is the new covenant fulfillment of the Passover.[37] Additionally, a more recent

---

36. Syd Hielema, former Director of Faith Formation in the CRC, in an email from December 14, 2018, commented "this is not an either—or; rather, the elders decide that the parents bear significant responsibility here, and find ways to support the parents in such discernment."

37. The first Passover was clearly a family meal and instructions were given that required the presence of children once the Israelites were settled in the promised land (Exod 12: 25–27). Later, however, only men (apparently including boys able to travel) were to go to the temple in Jerusalem for Passover (Deut 16:16). See Nicoletti, "Infant Baptism," 278: "What we find in the Mishnah is that infants were considered fully initiated into the Jewish religion from infancy, and were only hindered from participating in the religious life of the community to the extent that they were physically unable to do so. *Hagigah* 1:1 discusses at what age a boy was obligated to travel to Jerusalem to take part in the three annual feasts." (The Mishnah, it should be said, was not compiled in

interpretation of 1 Corinthians 11 points out that the sin being addressed was that of excluding certain members (the poor) and thus sinning against the body of Christ (the church). The wrongfulness of excluding covenant children fits with this interpretation.[38]

It is not my intention to debate paedocommunion here, except to state that it is quite consistent with paedobaptism *provided the focus is on the status of the covenant child.*[39] However, I believe that the various internal debates and the differing positions taken on the status of baptized infants become moot if one shifts the attention away from the significance of baptism for infants to its significance for *believers and their children.* This makes it perfectly reasonable for infants to be baptized as part of a Christian family, but to make their own profession of faith in later years. That said, such a profession need not await adulthood or late teenage years, as has traditionally been the case in the CRC. The issue is not age but genuine faith and age-appropriate spiritual discernment, whether at six or sixty.

---

its present form until c. AD 200, but portions of the text likely originated in previous rabbinic periods.) On the other hand, building on Ridderbos, Estelle argues that while the Passover provided the *occasion* for the Lord's Supper, "it is not to be identified with it." Elements of the Passover were missing in Jesus' Last Supper with his disciples. The Lord's Supper, "far from merely fulfilling the Passover meal, actually fulfills the *entire* sacrificial system." Further, it has both a fulfillment aspect and a provisional aspect, anticipating the marriage supper of the Lamb in the coming kingdom of God, a kingdom that is already here in principle, but not yet fully realized. It is "an intrusion of the heavenly into the mundane, earthly sphere. The king has come." Estelle concludes that if this is true, then "the question of whether children were present or participated in religious meals that the Hebrews Scriptures describe" becomes moot. ("Passover and the Lord's Supper," 41, 33, 45 (italics original); Cf. Ridderbos, *Coming of the Kingdom*).

38. More developed arguments along these lines can be found in the Spring 2007 issue of the *Calvin Theological Seminary Forum*.

39. When the PCA General Assembly debated paedocommunion in 1988, it was presented with a majority report arguing that "the two sacraments are to be distinguished . . . because of the heightened fulfillment of the New Covenant." The minority report responded in part that "This is precisely what baptists have argued in denying the support for infant baptism which we derive from the connection between circumcision and baptism" (Gilchrist, *PCA Digest*, 512).

On its way to opening the Lord's Table to all children of believers based simply on their baptism as covenant children, the CRC encouraged the participation of children at younger ages than had been the norm. After its Synod 1995 adopted guidelines for preparing children to participate in the Lord's Supper, CRC Publications produced a suitable guidebook for pastors and elders. It claimed that,

> In this we actually return to the practice of the early Reformed churches. Children were admitted to the Lord's table as young as age ten. They were prepared for this by receiving instruction in the Apostles' Creed, the Decalogue, the Lord's Prayer, and the meaning of the sacraments. They celebrated their first communion upon making a public profession of faith.

The document then admits: "Public profession of faith has grown into a kind of graduation from formal instruction in the confessions of the church. It has become the means for young adults to pledge their agreement with church doctrine, and the way for them to express their willingness to assume adult responsibilities." The guidebook then lists four declarations first adopted by Synod 1988 "that shift our practice back to a more biblical approach . . ." The fourth declaration has to do with young adults undertaking adult responsibilities of membership (such as voting rights), usually at the age of eighteen. The other three are as follows:

> a. The church is warranted in admitting to the Lord's Supper covenant children who give evidence of faith and are able to discern the body and remember and proclaim the death of Jesus in celebrating the Lord's Supper.
> b. The church is to assure itself of such faith through a public profession of faith on the part of covenant children.
> c. Covenant children should be encouraged to make profession of faith as soon as they exhibit faith and are able to discern the body and remember and proclaim the death of Jesus in celebrating the Lord's Supper.

These are followed by detailed instructions for parents and elders, including a visit by the elders to the child and parent(s), and ascertaining the appropriate level of understanding required.[40] Such a practice, had it been continued, is entirely consistent with the view outlined in this study. It may also be relevant to point out that in some Baptist churches, children are often baptized at similarly early ages,[41] although Reformed Baptists generally prefer to wait for evidence of a more mature faith in the teen years at the earliest.[42]

---

40. Christian Reformed Church, *Children's Profession of Faith*, 7–8. See also Christian Reformed Church, *Acts of Synod* 1988, 558–60.

41. Vander Zee observes that it is "a rather common feature in Baptist churches that children as young as five and six years old are baptized upon their profession of faith. It seems to me a bit of a stretch to see these baptisms as valid just because they follow upon conversion and profession of faith." He goes on to point out that "faith at that stage in life is so immersed in the family's life and identity that it hardly qualifies as conversion in the usual way in which the term is used, a radical transformation of life and commitment. For many who grow up in Christian families, all their faith decisions are interwoven with family structures and identities" (*Christ, Baptism and the Lord's Supper*, 129).

42. Morell (a Reformed Baptist), in "Two Young to Dunk?," para. 3, states that "These days, it's common for people to get baptized at 10 or younger," but the evidence from times past (1700–1840) suggests that "people were ordinarily baptized in their late teens or early twenties."

6

Missionary Baptism and Evangelical Unity

THE VIEW OF INFANT baptism presented here is sometimes accused of saying more about what baptism is *not* than about what it *is*. For instance, William H. Willimon, who wrote *Remember Who You Are: Baptism, A Model for Christian Life,* when he was Dean of Duke University Chapel and Professor of Christian Ministry at Duke Divinity School, tells of having seminarians preach on baptism in one of his courses. Typically, he would hear something like: "Baptism is a rite which Jesus commanded us to do, but it means nothing if we do not understand what we are doing"; or "While baptism is important, it is ineffective unless we bring our baptized child to Sunday school"; or "Baptism means nothing unless we really feel it in our hearts"; or "Baptism means nothing for the child; it is mainly a little service of dedication for the parents." After a series of these sermons, Willimon would stand up in desperation and cry out, "Will anyone now tell me why Jesus would have been so thoughtless as to command us to do something so utterly ineffective and meaningless as baptism?"[1]

---

1. Willimon, *Remember Who You Are,* 32.

DAVID WRIGHT

Willimon has a point. In his dense but illuminating essay "Scripture and Evangelical Diversity with Special Reference to the Baptismal Divide," David Wright affirms his conviction, based on a study of Ephesians 4:4–6, that "the New Testament does not allow us to regard baptism as a second order issue, let alone an *adiaphoron*. Whether we call it a sacrament or an ordinance, we agree that it belongs to that very small category of acts that Jesus explicitly instructed his followers to perpetuate."[2] He notes the "exalted company 'one baptism' keeps—the Trinity and the constitutive spiritual qualities of faith and hope."[3] Wright finds the solution to "evangelical diversity" in a common *theology* rather than *administration* of baptism,

> the obvious elements of which would include: baptism's dominical status, its grounding in the once-for-all saving work of Christ, its incorporation of the baptized in the body of Christ through the Spirit, and its expression of a response of faith to the gospel of Christ's redemption as it is appropriated for the baptized.[4]

In this connection, he observes that since:

> all paedobatist churches also baptize some non-infants, who seek baptism on their own initiative and answer for themselves . . . these churches cannot afford to incorporate in their theology of baptism any elements that are applicable only to babies. So the helpless and unresponsive passivity of babies should not be made theologically integral to baptism. . . . Baptism administered to tiny babies may be an admirable testimony to "the priority of

---

2. Wright, *Infant Baptism*, 291. Wright takes note of Beasley-Murray, "announcing his conversion to the recognition of the legitimacy of infant baptism on the part of credobaptists." He fleshes this out in terms of "a view of infant baptism which sees it as attesting the beginning of the work of grace in the baptized, and a reconsideration of the relation of believers' children to Christ's salvation which appeals to 1 Corinthians 7:14" (294). Cf. Beasley-Murray, "Problem of Infant Baptism," 9.

3. Wright, *Infant Baptism*, 293.

4. Wright, *Infant Baptism*, 293.

grace over faith" . . . but if true of the baptismal experience at all, it is surely no less true of a believer's baptism.
Of ourselves we do not believe. . .[5]

Wright considers *infant* baptism to be among the *adiaphora*.
He regards infant baptism as consistent with Scripture but not required by it, on a level with differing forms of church government.
His primary concern is with the indiscriminate practice he was familiar with in the Church of Scotland and the Church of England,
or as he put it in his book, *What Has Infant Baptism Done to Baptism?*, the devaluation of the meaning of baptism as a consequence
of what "'the long reign of infant baptism' has done to baptism."[6]

In "Recovering Baptism for a New Age of Mission," Wright
spells out the terms that to his mind would alone justify the con-
tinuation of the practice. He lists six points. The first of these is that
"only those parents who are regularly worshiping church members
would expect to have their infants baptized." This is in fact the
practice in Reformed denominations with a stricter discipline than
either of the two mentioned above. The second point is the "adoption of a service or services to mark the birth of a child, to enable
ministers to escape from the straightjacket of an all-or-nothing
choice." Once again, Wright is thinking of situations involving parents, or perhaps grandparents, with little or no church connection.
But he adds that "biblical precedents are not hard to seek." This is
presumably a reference to the biblical justifications offered for baby
dedication (such as Hannah's dedication of Samuel, or the mothers bringing their children to be blessed by Jesus). To this could be
added Wright's own research into various forms of dedication in
the early church. Next comes the "unambiguous owning of baby
baptism as New Testament baptism—period." Wright sees "no
defensible future for a paedobaptism which cannot bear the full
weight of the New Testament's baptismal witness." This leads in the
next place to the "nurture of baptized children as members of the
church and the people of God," which includes "early admission
to the Lord's table as entirely consistent with such a stance. By one

5. Wright, *Infant Baptism*, 294.

6. Wright, *Infant Baptism*, 102.

Spirit they have been baptized into the one body of Christ; their full belonging is not a matter of hope or prospect, but of present enjoyment." Point number five involves the "making of baptism an explicit and frequent reference-point in Christian education from the earliest stages. The baptized must grow up knowing that they are in Christ by baptism, that in baptism they died and rose again with Christ, and that through baptism they are his forever." The final point is that baptism should be a congregational rather than a family event.[7]

Several of these points are uncontroversial. They simply amount to parents taking seriously the commitments involved in the baptism of their children. However, in points three, four, and five, Wright's proper concern to take seriously the New Testament teaching on baptism leads him to apply to babies and young children all that baptism represents. I cannot see how this is consistent with his earlier claim that "Placing the theological rationale for baby baptism somewhere lower on the scale of credenda should enable us to tackle its discontents with greater freedom of movement."[8] Nor do I understand how it aids what in "Scripture and Evangelical Diversity" Wright applauds as the attractiveness of recent attempts to bridge the "waters that divide" in that:

> they penetrate behind divergent practice and dare to claim that both administrations of baptism can be embraced within one theological framework with little remainder. The one baptizes believers' babies and nurtures them within the community of faith until they profess that faith responsibly for themselves. The other dedicates or gives thanks for believers' babies and nurtures them within the community of faith until in baptism they respond to the gospel in their own profession. For both categories of baptismal subjects the prospective perspective is critical, both from an early acknowledgment of a child as God's gift to be reared in and to faith, and from

---

7. Wright, *Infant Baptism*, 375.

8. Wright, *Infant Baptism*, 372.

the later time of responsible decision, which is not so
much an arrival as a fresh point of departure.[9]

The mention of baby dedication here is not the same as a
minister finding an alternative ceremony for parents who wish
their child to be "done." It is a serious commitment of believing
parents to dedicate their children to God and bring them up in the
"teaching and instruction of the Lord" (Eph 6:4 ESV). Parents of
baptized infants make the same commitment. This is not to say
that infant baptism is no more than "baby dedication with water,"
but it is at least that. I believe that a greater stress on this "second
half" of baptism than is often common in Reformed churches is
both consistent with the pattern of household baptisms in the New
Testament and much more likely than Wright's proposal to dispel
misconceptions and thus bring real unity to congregations that allow for both practices.

Wright, as we saw earlier, accused Cunningham (and to a
lesser extent Bannerman) of having set the stage for a "base" view
of baptism in the Scottish church. But this need not be. I would
suggest that Cunningham's, rather than Wright's, view of infant
baptism is more consistent with the missionary baptism of the New
Testament and more hopeful for promoting its "one Lord, one faith,
one baptism" (Eph 4:5).

To be clear, I am not advocating a broad ecumenicity in
which central doctrines of the faith are negotiable. But within the
bounds of evangelical orthodoxy, it should be possible to arrive at
an understanding of the meaning of baptism that accommodates
the practice of infant baptism (as understood by Cunningham
and others) along with believers' baptism, with or without infant
dedication, for those not so convinced. The late great D. Martyn
Lloyd-Jones (1899–1981) gave three addresses in 1971 on "What is
an Evangelical?" First, he made clear those biblical doctrines that
he considered nonnegotiable for evangelicals. Then he turned to
what he considered nonessentials on which evangelicals should
unite. Among these were "the age and the mode of baptism." Lloyd-
Jones continued, "I have been reading books on this subject for the

---

9. Wright, *Infant Baptism*, 295.

last forty-four years and more, and I know less about it now than I did at the beginning. Therefore, when I assert, and we must all assert, that we believe in baptism, for that is plainly commanded, yet we must not divide and separate over the age of the candidate or over the mode of administration."[10] Reformed theologian John Frame makes a similar point in his *Evangelical Reunion: Denominations and the Body of Christ,* when he says, "Surely it would not be a breach of decency and order if a Presbyterian Church were to merge with a Baptist Church and keep a roll of members 'and their children,' leaving open (i.e., tolerating a difference as to) the actual status of these children, and allowing each family (or congregation within a denomination) to practice its own convictions as to whether or not the children should be baptized."[11] I rest my case!

Also, I agree with Ken Stewart (and Cunningham) that if the church as a whole were more missionary-minded, we would see more household baptisms such as took place in New Testament times. Further, the view of infant baptism presented in this book should ideally remove the scruples of those who have (rightly) rejected a different understanding. But we do not yet live in a perfect church.

LEONARD VANDER ZEE

In chapter 1, I indicated my desire to provide a corrective to the legacy of presumptive regeneration in the CRC. I also noted that the CRC no longer *officially* holds to that position, but that it has in fact been affirmed rather than repudiated in practice. A contemporary CRC leader, Leonard Vander Zee, in his highly acclaimed *Christ, Baptism and the Lord's Supper,* offers an interesting mix of endorsing the traditional view with one that is more open to other perspectives, indicative of some of the diversity that has arisen in recent years. He states (contrary to the position I have been advocating) that, "If infant baptism cannot be supported on the same basis and with the same understanding as adult baptism, then it is

---

10. Lloyd-Jones, "What Is an Evangelical?," 353.

11. Frame, *Evangelical Reunion*, 100.

unacceptable."[12] The subtitle of Vander Zee's book is *Recovering the Sacraments for Evangelical Worship*. Despite this, and some helpful material on the role of sacraments as symbols rather than simply signs (symbols "participate in the reality for which they stand"[13]), the author's overall approach is more likely to resonate with those of high church liturgical traditions than with most evangelicals whom he accuses of "deist rationalism and gnostic dualism," as well as "a docetic Jesus whose divinity tends to overshadow his humanity and who only brushes against creation for a time to lift (or rapture) us to heavenly safety."[14] As he writes in another connection, "This is not language designed to promote dialogue."[15] (The same might be said of his treatment of the Lord's Supper, which regularly blames Zwingli for evangelicals' devaluation of this sacrament[16] and, in his rightful desire to elevate the place of the Lord's Supper, downplays the centrality of the preached word in the Reformed understanding of the relationship between word and sacrament, but this section includes an excellent chapter on the history of debate around the meaning of the Eucharist. Vander Zee also makes a compelling case for weekly celebration.)

That said, and apart from Vander Zee's endorsement of presumptive regeneration and his qualified use of the common argument that infant baptism is uniquely suited to illustrate divine

---

12. Vander Zee, *Christ, Baptism and the Lord's Supper*, 121. This book received a "Book of the Year" award in its category from *Christianity Today* in 2005.

13. Vander Zee, *Christ, Baptism and the Lord's Supper*, 33, referencing Calvin's *Institutes*, 4.17.32.

14. Vander Zee, *Christ, Baptism and the Lord's Supper*, 16–17. Deist rationalism means belief in a God who is uninvolved with his creation. Gnostic dualism and Docetism are ancient heresies that separate the physical and spiritual, such that Christ's body was not really human, and thus his sufferings were only apparent. This is not modern evangelicalism by any stretch of the imagination, but to the extent that evangelicalism seems to stress the spiritual over against the physical (as in the goodness of creation and the physicality of the sacraments) it gives rise to these extravagant charges.

15. The context is the Heidelberg Catechism's condemnation of the Mass as a "condemnable idolatry" (Vander Zee, *Christ, Baptism and the Lord's Supper*, 205).

16. See footnote 13 in ch. 3 as to why this evaluation of Zwingli may be debatable.

grace,[17] I find relatively little to argue with in his doctrine of baptism as a whole. I was also pleasantly surprised to discover that after all is said and done, "we should not insist upon [infant baptism]." Referring to his own experience as a pastor (at the time of writing) to people from many different Christian backgrounds, Vander Zee notes, "I also find that we learn from one another. Baptists express respect for the covenantal aspects of the faith they learn in the practice of infant baptism. Paedobaptists learn to stress to their children the importance of their faith response to baptism."[18] I also agree with the observation about the "absurdly small amount of water" that is often used in infant baptism.[19]

Besides, in his discussion of household baptism, Vander Zee notes:

> It is interesting that in many mission situations today where Christianity encounters cultures where the social structures of the family and clan are deeply imbedded, baptism often involves whole groups. The chief, the head of the clan, or the family head becomes a believer, and all those under his authority (usually) follow. Rather than seeing this as an aberration from the normative individual response to the gospel (in Western culture), Acts suggests that we should see it as the way in which God by his Spirit naturally works through the social structures he has created.[20]

---

17. "We presume that all who are baptized are spiritually united with Christ, unless and until. . ." (Vander Zee, *Christ, Baptism and the Lord's Supper*, 113). This is said in the context of baptismal theology as a whole, but it clearly applies to infants, given that (according to Vander Zee) the meaning of the sacrament is the same for professing believers and baptized infants. "In baptism, as in salvation itself, human activity can only be a response to God's prior grace. That, in itself, is not an adequate defense of infant baptism, but it does at least lay a foundation on which to build one" (123). "The sacrament points to God's faithfulness more than to human faith. In that sense, infant baptism beautifully pictures what all baptisms are really about. . ." (131).

18. Vander Zee, *Christ, Baptism and the Lord's Supper*, 133.

19. Vander Zee, *Christ, Baptism and the Lord's Supper*, 71. See also, "The fact is, there is no airtight case for infant baptism" (122).

20. Vander Zee, *Christ, Baptism and the Lord's Supper*, 99.

There are potential dangers of religious nominalism in this approach (as there have been in the Constantinian past of Christendom), but *to the extent that* it reflects the biblical pattern of household/missionary baptism, I think perhaps, on this point, Cunningham might have approved.

DAVID FEDDES

A welcome approach somewhat in line with the one being advocated here is offered by another contemporary CRC leader, David Feddes, who was English Broadcast Minister of the CRC's *Back to God Hour* (now ReFrame Ministries) from 1990–2005. On January 6, 2002, Feddes delivered a powerful evangelistic message on "Baptism and New Life," stressing the connection between baptism and new life in Christ. He made no mention at all of infant baptism, but followed up the next week with "Should Babies Be Baptized?" Here, Feddes gave a fairly typical paedobaptist argument including the circumcision/baptism analogy and the household baptisms in the New Testament, based on the sermon text, Acts 16:33, "He and all his family were baptized" (NIV). However, he also stressed the need for personal faith in a way that is not always typical: "To be born into a Christian family and be baptized as a baby is no substitute for personal faith; it makes the call for personal faith all the more powerful and urgent."[21] Further, Feddes introduced his sermon with some important qualifications on Christian unity.[22] This chapter will close with that introduction:

> Should babies be baptized or not? It can be dangerous to
> ask that question. One danger is that Christians might
> be divided against each other. Christians don't all agree
> about infant baptism, so if they focus more on this area
> of disagreement than on their unity in Jesus Christ, it can

21. Feddes, "Should Babies Be Baptized?," para. 42.

22. "Should Babies Be Baptized?" was preached on the *Back to God Hour* on January 13, 2002. See also Feddes, "Baptism and the New Life," based on Titus 3:5, delivered the previous week, January 6, 2002. Both messages are available as recommended reading on a denominational website, but I would argue that they are not typical of at least traditional CRC practice.

cause division. A second, related danger is that if Christians disagree openly with each other, it can become an excuse for non-Christians to ignore Jesus and the Bible. Why pay attention to Christianity if Christians can't agree among themselves what to believe?

Recognizing these dangers, I don't want to say anything that sets Christians against each other or that repels people who don't yet know Jesus as their Savior. I love my fellow Christians and want to encourage deeper unity in Christ. I also love people who don't follow Christ, and I want each of you to enter a joyous, life-giving relationship with him. Above all, I love Jesus, and I want to honor him and draw people to him. So before I say whether babies should be baptized, a matter on which Christians don't all agree, I first want to emphasize common ground and highlight things on which all true Christians agree.

All true Christians believe the Bible as the Word of God. All true Christians believe in God the Father as Creator of the universe and Father of his people. All true Christians believe in Jesus as the Son of God and the Savior of all who trust in him. All true Christians believe in the Holy Spirit as the third Person of the Trinity, who connects us with Christ, produces faith, and gives eternal life. All true Christians believe that each person added to the Lord's church should be baptized in the name of the Father and of the Son and of the Holy Spirit.

All true Christians see baptism as a sign of sins being washed away and of being united with Christ's death and resurrection. All true Christians see baptism as a seal of God's grace for sinners, not of our own goodness. All true Christians see baptism as a mark by which God claims a person and requires faith, love, and obedience. All true Christians believe that an unbaptized person who has grown up outside a Christian setting, without faith in Christ, must turn to Jesus in repentance and personal faith before being baptized.

Not all Christians agree on whether babies born to believing parents should be baptized, but Christians do agree that it's a huge privilege and responsibility when a child is born into a Christian family. Even many who don't support infant baptism still have ceremonies of dedication in which they celebrate God's goodness and promise to lead their little one in God's ways.

Not all Christians agree on whether a personal, public commitment to Christ is necessary before a child from a Christian family is baptized, but Christians do agree that such a personal, public commitment is necessary at some point. Even those who support infant baptism still insist that those who are baptized as babies must later respond with a public profession of personal faith in Christ as Lord and Savior, and must live for him.

Christians may have differences, but let's never forget the common ground and the unity Christians share. . .[23]

---

23. Feddes, "Should Babies Be Baptized?," paras. 1–8.

7

Conclusion

In chapter 1, I introduced the different views of infant baptism from my Scottish Highland background and my current ministry in a branch of Dutch Reformed Christianity. I also referenced another branch of the Dutch Reformed Church, closer to my own background, in the person of Joel Beeke. I returned to Beeke in chapter 5 to discuss the status of believers' children. In between, the two longest chapters were devoted to the baptismal views of a Lowland, nineteenth-century Scot, William Cunningham, and their present-day implications. Cunningham's view differed from the Highland one only in that he did not make a distinction between the faith required for baptism (whether as a convert or a parent) and for admission to the Lord's Table.

Prior to introducing Cunningham, I referenced Ken Stewart's essay, "Early Church Baptism in the Hands of Evangelical Protestants." Stewart's contribution to the baptismal debate reflected the influence of Everett Ferguson and David Wright, both of whom raised questions about the historicity of infant baptism in the early church. He (Stewart) expressed his sense of chagrin that this research had not had more influence on his fellow paedobaptists and argued for a "more modest"[1] modification of the doctrine. Of a few options available, he recommended renewed attention to the

---

1. Stewart, *In Search of Ancient Roots*, 139.

household baptisms of the New Testament. This I have attempted to do, calling them *missionary baptisms* since they involved new converts and their households undergoing the rite of admission into the Christian church. I also noted Cunningham's point that if we were more in the habit of witnessing the baptisms of converts (and their households) on the mission field, we would be more inclined to understand that what he called adult (i.e., believers' or converts') baptism was the biblical norm.

Along the way, I paid attention to another of Stewart's suggested options, as advocated by Tony Lane and David Wright: the dual practice of infant and believers' baptism, the latter usually (but not necessarily) also involving baby dedication as an alternative to infant baptism. Examples were given from history, as well as the present, of churches that have adopted this practice, at least in theory. Of course, churches that regularly practice infant baptism also admit older converts by way of baptism, but what is being advocated is more than that. It is the coexistence and acceptance of different views of baptism in one church. The underlying conviction is that Jesus' prayer for visible unity in John 17 and Paul's affirmation of "one Lord, one faith, one baptism" (Eph 4:5) requires this.

Some (probably many) would consider such a proposal impractical, even naïve, but my argument is that a view of infant baptism more like Cunningham's than others (presumptive election or regeneration) makes this more feasible, and is in fact the only way to do so. My appeal is to the broader evangelical church, where baby dedication is common, but as a member of the Reformed community, the closest connection is with Reformed Baptists. Because, like other Reformed folk, they stress the priority of divine grace in salvation, Reformed Baptists are less likely than other evangelicals to practice baby dedication, which is seen to be more of a human response than a divine initiative. I noticed, however, how at least some of their number found Cunningham's view of baptism to be closer to their own than that of other paedobaptists. This was a point of criticism for Letham, but I would argue it should be a basis for greater unity, specifically in the Reformed community, as well as beyond it.

William Barker, in a helpful critique of this study in manuscript form, notes, "It is natural in America for Reformed and Presbyterian evangelicals to seek unity with Reformed Baptists, with whom we have so much in common. But there are also Lutherans and Anglicans with whom Reformed evangelicals have much in common."[2] This is true. My focus has been on the relationship between believers' and infant baptism, which is why I single out Reformed Baptists, with whom I partially agree. In doing so, I have quoted one of the foremost Anglican leaders of the last century, the late J. I. Packer, whose influence is reflected in the view I have presented. Others (e.g., John Stott, whom I also reference), defend infant baptism more along the traditional line that "a sacrament is a sign not of what we do or are, but of what God has done or does."[3] True as this statement is in general, I suggested that the ensuing argument is nowhere made directly in the New Testament and that therefore (with David Wright) "the helpless and unresponsive passivity of babies should not be made theologically integral to baptism."[4] I am not naïve or arrogant enough (I hope) to think that all evangelical Anglicans and Lutherans, or even Baptists and Presbyterians, let alone my colleagues in the CRC, will be convinced by my argument. Still, one has to start somewhere.

Meanwhile, it seems fitting to end for now with a quotation from one of Cunningham's colleagues, the beloved John ("Rabbi") Duncan (1796–1870), who served as a missionary to Jews in Hungary before taking the chair of Hebrew and Oriental Languages at New College, Edinburgh in 1843. One of the many aphorisms for which he is remembered sums up the spirit of what has been attempted here: "I am first a Christian, next a catholic, then a Calvinist, fourth a paedobaptist, and fifth a Presbyterian. I cannot reverse this order."[5]

---

2. Barker, email, May 10, 2021.
3. Stott and Motyer, *Anglican Evangelical Doctrine of Infant Baptism*, 7.
4. Wright, *Infant Baptism*, 294
5. Knight, *Colloquia Peripatetica*, 8.

Bibliography

Aland, Kurt. *Did the Early Church Baptize Infants?* Translated by G. K. Beasley-Murray. London: SCM, 1961.

Alexander, Archibald. *Thoughts on Religious Experience.* 1884. Reprint, Edinburgh: Banner of Truth, 1978.

Bannerman, James. *The Church of Christ*, Vol 2. 2 vols. Edinburgh: T. & T. Clark, 1868.

Barcellos, Richard, ed., *Recovering a Covenantal Heritage: Essays in Baptist Covenant Theology.* Self-published: Create Space, 2014.

Barth, Karl. *Church Dogmatics.* 5 vols. Translated by G. W. Bromiley. Edinburgh: T. & T. Clark, 1969.

———. *Learning Jesus through the Heidelberg Catechism.* Translated by Shirley J. Guthrie Jr. Grand Rapids: Eerdmans, 1982.

———. *The Teaching of the Church Regarding Baptism.* Translated by Ernest E. Payne. London: SCM, 1948.

Bavinck, Herman. *Reformed Dogmatics.* Vol 4. 4 vols. Edited by John Bolt. Translated by John Vriend. Grand Rapids: Baker Academic, 2008.

———. *Saved by Grace: The Holy Spirit's Work in Calling and Regeneration.* Edited by J. Mark Beach. Translated by Nelson D. Kloosterman. Grand Rapids: Reformation Heritage, 2008.

Baxter, Richard. *The Practical Works of Richard Baxter*, Vol 1: *A Christian Directory etc.* 4 vols. 1673. Reprint, Ligonier, PA: Soli Deo Gloria, 1990.

———. *Rich. Baxter's review* (sic) *of the State of Christian Infants etc.* London: Nevil Simons, 1676.

Beach, J. Mark. "Abraham Kuyper, Herman Bavinck and 'The Conclusions of Utrecht.'" *Mid-America Journal of Theology* 19 (2008) 11–68.

Beasley-Murray, George R. *Baptism in the New Testament.* Grand Rapids: Eerdmans, 1972.

———. "The Problem of Infant Baptism: An Exercise in Possibilities." In *Festschrift Günther Wagner*, edited by Faculty of Baptist Theological Seminary, Rüschlikon, 1–14. International Theological Studies 1. New York: Lang, 1994.

Beeke, Joel R. *Bringing the Gospel to Covenant Children*. Grand Rapids: Reformation Heritage, 2010.

————. *Parenting by God's Promises: How to Raise Children in the Covenant of Grace*. Sanford, FL: Reformation Trust, 2011.

Bierma, Lyle, D. *German Calvinism in the Confessional Age: The Covenant Theology of Caspar Olevianus*. Grand Rapids: Baker, 1997.

Boersma, Hans. *Richard Baxter's Understanding of Infant Baptism*. Studies in Reformed Theology and History 7. Princeton: Princeton Theological Seminary Press, 2002.

Bonhoeffer, Dietrich. *The Cost of Discipleship*. 1959. Reprint, New York: Simon and Schuster, 1995.

The Book of Church Order of the Presbyterian Church in America. Sixth edition. Decatur, GA: Office of the Stated Clerk, 2017.

Bradshaw, P. F., et al. *The Apostolic Tradition: A Commentary*. Hermeneia. Minneapolis: Fortress, 2002.

Bratt, James D., ed. *Abraham Kuyper: A Centennial Reader*. Grand Rapids: Eerdmans, 1998.

Bruce, F. F. *The Acts of the Apostles*. 3rd rev. ed. Grand Rapids: Eerdmans, 1990.

Calvin, John. *Institutes of the Christian Religion*, Vol 2. 3 vols. Translated by Henry Beveridge. Edinburgh: Calvin Translation Society, 1845.

Campbell, Iain D., and Malcolm Maclean, eds. *The People's Theologian: Writings in Honour of Donald Macleod*. Fearn, UK: Christian Focus, 2011.

Cassidy, James J. "Calvin on Baptism: Baptismal Regeneration or the *Duplex Loquiende Modus*?" In *Resurrection and Redemption, Theology in Service of the Church: Essays in Honor of Richard B. Gaffin Jr.*, edited by Lane G. Tipton & Jeffrey C. Waddington, 534–54. Phillipsburg, NJ: P & R, 2008.

Catechism of the Catholic Church. New York: Doubleday, 1995.

Christian Reformed Church. *Acts of Synod*. Grand Rapids: CRC, 1908.

————. *Acts of Synod*. Grand Rapids: CRC, 1968.

————. *Acts of Synod*. Grand Rapids: CRC, 1988.

————. *Acts of Synod*. Grand Rapids: CRC, 2007.

————. *Acts of Synod*. Grand Rapids: CRC, 2011.

————. *Agenda for Synod*. Grand Rapids: CRC, 2011.

————. *Children's Profession of Faith*. Grand Rapids: CRC, 1996.

Church of Scotland. *Interim Report of the Special Commission on Baptism*. Edinburgh: St. Andrew, 1958.

Collins, C. John. "What Does Baptism Do for Anyone?" *Presbyterion* (Spring and Fall, 2012) 1–31, 74–98.

Cottrell, Jack W. "Zwingli's Covenant Theology and the Reformed Doctrine of Baptism." Evangelical Theological Society Papers, 38th Annual Conference, 1986.

"Council of Trent: Session 7 Canon 8." https://www.papalencyclicals.net/councils/trent/seventh-session.htm.

Cunningham, William. *Historical Theology*, Vol 2, second edition. 2 vols. Edinburgh: T. & T. Clark, 1864.

———. "Zwingli and the Sacraments." In *The Reformers and the Theology of the Reformation*, by William Cunningham, 212–91. Edinburgh: T. & T. Clark, 1866.

Dabney, R. L. "The Changes Proposed in Our Book of Discipline." *The Southern Presbyterian Review* 12.1 (April 1859) 36–83.

de Fleury, Maria. *Hymns for Believer's Baptism*. London: Justins, 1786.

DeMoor, Henry. *Christian Reformed Church Order Commentary*. Grand Rapids: Faith Alive Christian Resources, 2010.

de Witt, John R. "Children and the Covenant of Grace: A Review Article." *Westminster Theological Journal* 37.2 (Winter 1975) 239–45.

Douma, J. *Infant Baptism and Regeneration*. Kampen, the Netherlands: Self-published, 1976.

Dunn, James D. G. *Baptism in the Holy Spirit*. London: SCM, 1970.

Estelle, Bryan D. "Passover and the Lord's Supper: Continuity or Discontinuity?" In *Children and the Lord's Supper*, edited by Guy Walters and Ligon Duncan, 31–57. Fearn, UK: Christian Focus, 2011.

Feddes, David. "Baptism and the New Life." https://new.crcna.org/welcome/beliefs/position-statements/baptism/baptism-and-new-life.

———. "Should Babies Be Baptized?" https://new.crcna.org/welcome/beliefs/position-statements/baptism/should-babies-be-baptized.

Ferguson, Everett. *Baptism in the Early Church*. Grand Rapids: Eerdmans, 2009.

Ferguson, Sinclair B. *John Owen on the Christian Life*. Edinburgh: Banner of Truth, 1987.

Finn, Nathan A. "Was John Bunyan a Baptist? An Exercise in Historical Method." http://andrewfullercenter.org/articles/blog/2014/07/was-john-bunyan-a-baptist-a-test-case-in-historical-method.

Frame, John M. *Evangelical Reunion: Denominations and the Body of Christ*. Grand Rapids: Baker, 1991.

Gilchrist, Paul R., ed. *PCA Digest: Position Papers 1973–1993*, Part 5. 5 parts. Atlanta: Presbyterian Church in America, 1993.

Hammann, G. *Entre la secte et la cite. Le project d'église du réformateur Martin Bucer (1491–1551)*. Geneva: n.p., 1984.

Hodge, Charles. "The Church Membership of Infants." *Biblical Repertory and Princeton Review* 30.2 (April 1858) 347–89.

———. "The General Assembly." *Biblical Repertory and Princeton Review* 31.3 (1859) 533–70.

———. *Systematic Theology*, Vol 3. 3 vols. Grand Rapids: Scribner, Armstrong, 1872.

Hoeksema, Herman. *Believers and Their Seed: Children in the Covenant*. Grand Rapids: Reformed Free Publishing Association, 1971.

———. *The Triple Knowledge: An Exposition of the Heidelberg Catechism*. Vol 1. 10 vols. Grand Rapids: Reformed Free Publishing Association, 1970.

Hoffeker, W. Andrew. *Piety and the Princeton Theologians: Archibald Alexander, Charles Hodge and Benjamin Warfield*. Phillipsburg, NJ: P & R, 1981.

Jeremias, Joachim. *Infant Baptism in the First Four Centuries*. Translated by Dorothy M. Barton. London: SCM, 1971.

———. *The Origins of Infant Baptism*. Translated by David Cairns. London: SCM, 1962.

Jewett, Paul K. *Infant Baptism and Confirmation*. Pasadena, CA: Fuller Theological Seminary Press, 1960.

———. *Infant Baptism and the Covenant of Grace*. Grand Rapids: Eerdmans, 1978.

Keefe, Susan A. *Water and the Word: Baptism and the Education of the Clergy in the Carolingian Empire*. Vol 2. 2 vols. Notre Dame, IN: University of Notre Dame Press, 2002.

Kennedy, John. *The Days of the Fathers in Ross-shire*. Edinburgh: n.p., 1897.

Kingdon, David. *Children of Abraham*. Sussex, UK: Carey, 1973.

Kline, Meredith G. *By Oath Consigned: A Reinterpretation of the Covenant Signs of Circumcision and Baptism*. Grand Rapids: Eerdmans, 1968.

Klooster, Fred. *Our Only Comfort: A Comprehensive Commentary on the Heidelberg Catechism*. Vol 2. 2 vols. Grand Rapids: Faith Alive, 2001.

Knight, William *Colloquia Peripatetica*. 5th ed. Edinburgh: Douglas, 1879.

Koeman, Ken. "Q & A Page." *The Banner* (August 18 1997) 23.

Kolb, Robert. "God's Baptismal Act as Regenerative." In *Understanding Four Views on Baptism*, edited by John H. Armstrong, 91–109. Grand Rapids: Zondervan, 2007.

Kuyper, A. "Calvinism and Confessional Revision." *The Presbyterian Quarterly* 4.18 (October 1891) 369–99.

Letham, Robert. "Book Review: *The People's Theologian: Writings in Honour of Donald Macleod*." *Foundations* 61 (Autumn 2011) 74–77.

———. *The Water That Unites*. Fearn, UK: Christian Focus, 2012.

Letham, Robert, and Donald Macleod. "Is Evangelicalism Christian?" *Evangelical Quarterly* 67.1 (Jan-March 1995) 3–33.

Lloyd-Jones, D. Martyn. "What Is an Evangelical?" In *Knowing the Times: Addresses Delivered on Various Occasions, 1942–1977*, by D. Martyn Lloyd-Jones, 299–355. Edinburgh: Banner of Truth, 1989.

Lusk, Rich. "Do I Believe in Baptismal Regeneration?" https://www.trinity-pres.net/essays/do-I-believe-in-baptismal-regeneration.pdf.

———. "From Birmingham with Love: A Federal Vision Postcard." In *A Faith That Is Never Alone: A Response to Westminster Seminary California*, edited by P. Andrew Sandlin, 109–61. La Grange, CA: Kerygma, 2007.

Macleod, Donald. *A Faith to Live By: Understanding Christian Doctrine*. Second Edition. Fearn, UK: Mentor, 2010.

———. "Scotland's Greatest Theologian." *The Monthly Record of the Free Church of Scotland* (March 1990) 51–53.

———. "Should Presbyterians Have Dedication Services?" www.donaldmacleod. org.uk/dm/should-presbyterians-have-dedication-services/.

Macleod, John. *Scottish Theology in relation* (sic) *to Church History*. 1943. Reprint, Edinburgh: Knox and Banner of Truth, 1974.

Migliore, D. L. *Faith Seeking Understanding*. Grand Rapids: Eerdmans, 1991.

Morell, Caleb. "Too Young to Dunk? An Examination of Baptists and Baptismal Ages, 1700–1840." 9Marks, June 21, 2021. www.9marks.org/article/too-young-to-dunk-an-examination-of-baptists-and-baptismal-ages-1700-1840/.

Murray, John. *Christian Baptism*. 1952. Reprint, Philadelphia: Presbyterian and Reformed, 1974.

Najapfour, Brian G. *Child Dedication Considered Historically, Theologically, and Pastorally*. Caledonia, MI: Biblical Spirituality, 2014.

Nicoletti, Steven A. "Infant Baptism in the First-Century Presuppositional Pool." *Tyndale Bulletin* 66.2 (2015) 271–92.

Orme, William. *Bibliotheca Biblica: A Select List of Books of Sacred Literature with Notices Biographical, Critical and Bibliographical*. Edinburgh: Adam Black, 1824.

Packer. J. I. *Concise Theology: A Guide to Historic Christian Beliefs*. Carol Stream, IL: Tyndale House, 2001.

———. *The Redemption and Restoration of Man in the Thought of Richard Baxter*. Vancouver: Regent College Publishing, 2013.

———. "The Uniqueness of Jesus Christ: Some Evangelical Reflections." *Churchman* 92.2 (1978) 101–11.

Pearse, Meic. *The Great Restoration: The Religious Radicals of the 16th and 17th Centuries*. Carlisle, UK: Paternoster, 1998.

Puritan Board. "William Cunningham on Baptism." https://www.puritanboard.com/threads/william-cunningham-on-baptism.2730/.

Rainey, Robert, and James Mackenzie. *Life of William Cunningham, D.D.* 1871. Reprint, London: Forgotten, 2015.

Rayburn, Robert. *What about Baptism?* 1957. Reprint, Grand Rapids: Baker, 1979.

Ridderbos, Herman. *The Coming of the Kingdom*. Phillipsburg, NJ: Presbyterian and Reformed, 1962.

Robertson, David. "The Downgrade of the Free Church–A Response to Donald Macleod." https://theweeflea.com/2017/08/12/the-downgrading-of-the-free-church-a-response-to-donald-macleod/.

———. "When the Levy Breaks–Is Dedicating an Infant, Covenant Breaking?" https://theweeflea.com/2017/07/26/when-the-levy-breaks-is-dedicating-an-infant-covenant-breaking?

Schenck, Lewis Bevens. *The Presbyterian Doctrine of Children in the Covenant: An Historical Study of the Significance of Infant Baptism in the Presbyterian Church*. 1940. Reprint, Phillipsburg, NJ: P & R, 2003.

Schreiner, Thomas R., & Shawn D. Wright, eds. *Believer's Baptism: Sign of the New Covenant in Christ*. Nashville, TN: B & H Academic 2007.

Scott, James W. "The Biblical Basis for Infant Baptism." *New Horizons in the Orthodox Presbyterian Church*. opc.org/nh.html?article_id=276dication.

Smallman, Stephen. *How Our Children Come to Faith*. Phillipsburg, NJ: P & R, 2006.

BIBLIOGRAPHY

Stewart, Kenneth J. *In Search of Ancient Roots: The Christian Past and the Evangelical Identity Crisis*. Downers Grove, IL: InterVarsity, 2017.

———. "Review of Lewis B. Schenk, *The Presbyterian Doctrine of Children in the Covenant*." *Presbyterion: Covenant Seminary Review* 30.2 (2007) 124–26.

Stoppels, Sake. "Een kerk met gastvrije drempels." *Kerk en Theologie* 60.3 (2009) 234–38.

Stott, John, and Alec Motyer. *The Anglican Evangelical Doctrine of Infant Baptism*. London: The Latimer Trust, 2008.

Strawbridge, Gregg, ed., *The Case for Covenantal Infant Baptism*. Phillipsburg, NJ: P & R, 2003.

Tan, Simon G. H. "Reassessing Believer's Baptism in Pentecostal Theology and Practice." *Asian Journal of Pentecostal Studies* 6.2 (2003) 219–34.

Ursinus, Zacharias. *The Commentary of Zacharias Ursinus on the Heidelberg Catechism*. Translated by the Rev. G. W. Williard. 1852. Reprint, Phillipsburg, NJ: Presbyterian and Reformed, 1985.

van der Leer, Tuen. "The True Calvinist is a Baptist." *Baptist Quarterly* 44.1 (2011) 21–35.

Vander Zee, Leonard J. *Christ, Baptism and the Lord's Supper: Recovering the Sacraments for Evangelical Worship*. Wheaton, IL: InterVarsity Academic, 2004.

Van Dyke, Henry J. *The Church: Her Ministry and Sacraments: Lectures Delivered on the L. P. Stone Foundation at Princeton Theological Seminary in 1890*. New York: A. D. F. Randolph, 1890.

Warfield, B. B. "The Polemics of Infant Baptism." *The Presbyterian Quarterly* 13.48 (April 1899) 313–34.

Westminster Confession of Faith with the Larger and Shorter Catechisms. Inverness, UK: Committee of the Free Presbyterian Church of Scotland, 1970.

Williams, Andrew Ray. "Water Baptism in Pentecostal Perspective: A Bibliographic Evaluation." *Spiritus* 4.1 (Spring 2019) 68–91.

Willimon, William H. *Remember Who You Are: Baptism, a Model for Christian Life*. Nashville, TN: The Upper Room, 1980.

Wilson, Douglas. "Baptism and Children." In *The Case for Covenantal Infant Baptism*, edited by Gregg Strawbridge, 286–302. Phillipsburg, NJ: P & R, 2003.

———. *To a Thousand Generations: Infant Baptism-God's Covenant Mercy for the People of God*. Moscow, ID: Canon, 2000.

Wolters, Albert, "What Is to Be Done . . . Toward a Neo-Calvinist Agenda?" https://www.cardus.ca/comment/article/282/what-is-to-be-done-toward-a-neocalvinist-agenda/.

Wright, David F. ed., *Baptism: Three Views*. Downers Grove, IL: IVP Academic, 2009.

———. *Infant Baptism in Historical Perspective: Collected Studies*. Studies in Christian History and Thought. Milton Keynes, UK: Paternoster, 2007.

———. *What Has Infant Baptism Done to Baptism? An Enquiry at the End of Christendom*. Carlisle, UK: Paternoster, 2005.

Index

Index

Index

INDEX

Ingram Content Group UK Ltd.
Milton Keynes UK
UKHW022215110723
424974UK00004B/18

9 781666 720471